Study Guide
Leda Thompson
Kenrick S. Thompson
Arkansas State University Mountain Home

SOCIOLOGY
Social Life and Social Issues

Linda L. Lindsey
Maryville University

Stephen Beach
Kentucky Wesleyan College

PRENTICE HALL, Upper Saddle River, NJ 07458

ISBN-0-13-022360-3

Printed in the United States of America

TABLE OF CONTENTS

PREFACE/NOTE TO THE STUDENT

This *Study Guide* is designed for use with **SOCIOLOGY: SOCIAL LIFE AND SOCIAL ISSUES** by Linda L. Lindsey and Stephen Beach. There are five elements for each chapter in the text:

        1.   Learning Objectives
        2.   Chapter Outline
        3.   Summary
        4.   Multiple Choice Questions
        5.   True-False Questions

For each chapter, 20 sample multiple choice and 10 sample true-false questions are provided. The correct answers and page references for these items are listed at the conclusion of the chapter.

We hope that this *Study Guide* will be helpful to you in your study of social life and social issues. If you have any suggestions, please write to us or send an e-mail message.

Leda Thompson, M.A. and Kenrick S. Thompson, Ph.D.
Arkansas State University Mountain Home
1600 South College
Mountain Home, AR 72653
Internet Address: LTHOMPSON@BROOK.ASUMH.EDU
               or
        KTHOMPSON@BROOK.ASUMH.EDU

CHAPTER 1
THE SOCIOLOGICAL PERSPECTIVE

LEARNING OBJECTIVES

➤ To be able to define sociology and understand the sociological perspective.

➤ To learn to identify examples of the way social forces affect our everyday lives.

➤ To begin to see the conditions in society that encourage us to think sociologically about issues and problems in the world.

➤ To recognize the sociological perspective and the benefits to be gained from applying it to issues and problems.

➤ To be able to identify the important historical factors in the development of sociology.

➤ To be able to identify and distinguish among the functionalist, conflict and interactionist paradigms used by sociologists to examine society.

CHAPTER OUTLINE

I.   What is Sociology?

II.   The Sociological Perspective
        A. Sociology as Science
        B. The Debunking Theme
        C. Emphasis on Diversity
        D. Emphasis on Globalization

III.   Major Topics of Sociological Interest
        A. Socialization
        B. Structured Social Inequality
        C. Social Institutions
        D. Social Change

IV.   The Development of Sociology
        A. The Sociohistorical Context
        B. European Origins of Sociology
        C. Sociology in the United States

V.   Three Sociological Paradigms
        A. Functionalism
        B. Conflict Theory
        C. Symbolic Interactionism

VI.   The Uses of Sociology
        A. Improving Society
        B. Making a Living
        C. Making Life Choices

SUMMARY

> Sociology is a perspective or way of thinking that systematically addresses the impact of social forces on human behavior.

> Sociologists employ scientific research procedures in order to collect empirical data and construct theories that explain social reality as accurately as possible.

> Sociologists try to identify the hidden as well as the more obvious explanations of social behavior, a process called debunking.

> The discipline of sociology is strongly oriented toward the importance of cultural diversity and of the globalization process in explaining contemporary patterns of social life.

> Sociologists pay particular attention to four general aspects of social life: socialization, structured social inequality, social institutions, and social change.

> Sociology arose in Europe during the mid-nineteenth century; its development was encouraged by the expansion of science, the ideas of the Enlightenment, the Industrial Revolution, and the spread of colonialism.

> Key figures in the growth of sociology include Auguste Comte and Emile Durkheim in France, Karl Marx and Max Weber in Germany, and Herbert Spencer in England.

➢ Women and minorities, largely excluded from the discipline until recently, are now making substantial contributions.

➢ The functional paradigm analyzes how the various components of social systems work to keep them operating smoothly and efficiently and to avoid dramatic changes.

➢ The conflict paradigm maintains that social life is best understood as a struggle between competing individuals and groups for scarce and valued resources, and that change in social life is constant.

➢ The symbolic interactionist paradigm focuses at the microsociological level on how the meanings that people construct through interaction shape human social behavior.

➢ Sociology may be useful in helping people solve social problems, earn a living, and make major life decisions.

MULTIPLE CHOICE

1. The sociological perspective assumes that _____ factors are especially useful in explaining the regularities in the way people act.

   a. biological
   b. psychological
   c. social
   d. physiological

2. C. Wright Mills defined which of the following as an awareness of "the intersection between history and biography"?

   a. personal troubles
   b. the sociological imagination
   c. social issues
   d. the sociological perspective

3.   C. Wright Mills differentiated between _____, which result from individual
      failings, and _____, which are caused by larger social factors.

      a. personal troubles/social issues
      b. private woes/environmental realities
      c. imagined difficulties/social realities
      d. psychological ailments/social problems

4.   Which of the following is NOT distinctive about the sociological perspective?

      a. employment of scientific methods
      b. encouragement to debunk or be skeptical of conventional explanations of
         social life
      c. directs attention to social diversity
      d. displays a limited global orientation

5.   The term *empirical reality* refers to

      a. facts that can be apprehended directly by the senses.
      b. what is considered "best" by the majority.
      c. what is generally agreed upon by the majority.
      d. nonscientific observation.

6.   Which process allows researchers to apply the same fundamental explanations
      to many different specific cases?

      a. empirical observation
      b. scientific deduction
      c. generalization
      d. projection

7.   When sociologist Emile Durkheim showed that suicide stems not only from
      psychological problems, but also from low levels of social integration, he was

      a. projecting.
      b. debunking.
      c. hypothesizing.
      d. theorizing.

8. Through no necessary fault of his own, David is to some extent excluded from the mainstream of society. David displays which of the following qualities?

   a. gregariousness
   b. anxiety
   c. social marginality
   d. depression

9. Social organization involves the implicit social contract requiring that people learn and accept the rules that govern social behavior. The mechanism by which this learning is accomplished is termed

   a. social acquisition.
   b. social generalization.
   c. globalization.
   d. socialization.

10. Racism, sexism, and ageism are good examples of _____ that define structured social inequality as just and proper.

   a. ideologies
   b. edicts
   c. laws
   d. mores

11. A/an _____ is a predictable, established way to provide for one or more of society's basic needs.

   a. environment
   b. law
   c. social institution
   d. theory

12. Four key developments led ultimately to the birth of sociology. Which of the following is NOT one of these?

   a. Growing out of the Renaissance, scientific ways of investigating the natural world began to gain greater acceptance, despite the hostility of the church.
   b. In both politics and science, the notion spread that the human condition could and should be improved through the application of reason.
   c. Especially in the decades following 1880, colonialism rapidly expanded.
   d. During the 1800s, the expansion of industrial societies became extremely limited.

13. French sociologist Emile Durkheim used the term _____ in referring to a general decline in the strength of the rules that guide people in deciding how they should behave in society.

   a. anxiety
   b. anomie
   c. alienation
   d. *Gemeinschaft*

14. The sociologists within the "Chicago School" viewed their city as a kind of vast social laboratory, interpreting urban problems in the context of the physical growth of the metropolis. Their approach is termed

   a. urban ecology.
   b. gentrification.
   c. social Darwinism.
   d. positivism.

15. Which perspective interprets all social groups as *systems* whose parts are interdependent so that a change in one element necessarily leads to changes in every other element?

   a. symbolic interactionism
   b. conflict theory
   c. functionalism
   d. developmentalism

16. Some critics charge that the functional paradigm _____ the extent to which harmony and stability actually exist in society.

   a. ignores
   b. underestimates
   c. rejects
   d. overemphasizes

17. Which macrosociological paradigm is in many ways a mirror image of functionalism?

   a. conflict theory
   b. symbolic interactionism
   c. exchange theory
   d. developmentalism

18. Sociologists who favor _____ tend to believe that they should become actively involved in society, usually on the side of people who lack substantial social power.

   a. functionalism
   b. conflict theory
   c. symbolic interactionism
   d. developmentalism

19. The statement "If men [*sic*] define situations as real, they are real in their consequences" has become known as the _____ Theorem.

   a. Parsons
   b. Spencer
   c. Durkheim
   d. Thomas

20. An increasing number of sociologists believe that practitioners of the discipline should put their knowledge and skills to work in the real world. This orientation is called

   a. functionalism.
   b. developmentalism.
   c. applied sociology.
   d. environmentalism.

TRUE-FALSE

1. T A *theory* is an explanation of the relationship between specific facts.

2. F Once they are tested appropriately, theories in sociology are irrefutable.

3. F The *debunking* theme in sociology helps explain why sociology thrives during times of extreme calm and political conservatism.

4. F The division of people into several different social categories is a phenomenon that is found in a minority of world societies.

5. T Sociology is among the newest of sciences.

6. T Sociology began in France.

7. F Karl Marx's primary contributions to sociology include the idea that social life can best be viewed as an arena of consensus and cooperation.

8. T Herbert Spencer is probably best remembered for his philosophy of *social Darwinism*.

9. T Until the late 1930s, the "Chicago School" virtually dominated sociology in the United States.

10. F Functionalism and conflict theory are *microsociological* approaches.

ANSWERS - MULTIPLE CHOICE (correct answer/page reference)

1.	c	4
2.	b	5
3.	a	5
4.	d	5-6
5.	a	6
6.	c	6
7.	b	9
8.	c	10
9.	d	11
10.	a	12
11.	c	13
12.	d	14-15
13.	b	16
14.	a	17
15.	c	20
16.	d	21
17.	a	22
18.	b	23
19.	d	24
20.	c	26

ANSWERS - TRUE-FALSE (correct answer/page reference)

1.	T	7
2.	F	7
3.	F	9
4.	F	12
5.	T	13
6.	T	15
7.	F	16
8.	T	16
9.	T	17
10.	F	19

CHAPTER 2
THE RESEARCH PROCESS

LEARNING OBJECTIVES

➤ To identify the principals of the scientific method used by sociologists, including the meaning of objectivity, problem formulation, and hypothesis testing.

➤ To learn the basic methods of data collection: use of questionnaires, interviews, observation and documentary resources.

➤ To be able to identify the four basic research designs: experiments, surveys, secondary research, and field research.

➤ To be able to identify and explain the essential structure of the experiment and how it helps to establish causality.

➤ To be able to identify the advantages and disadvantages of the survey design.

➤ To learn the types of secondary data analysis using archives, documents, government statistics and public opinion polls.

➤ To become aware of the ethical problems associated with doing sociological research.

CHAPTER OUTLINE

I.   Research and the Science of Sociology

II.   Steps in the Research Process
        A. Formulating the Problem
        B. Measurement
        C. Collecting Data
        D. Analyzing and Interpreting Data

III.   Research Designs
        A. Experimental Designs
        B. Surveys
        C. Secondary Research
        D. Field Research

SUMMARY

➤ Sociologists use the scientific method to test, modify and develop their theories. As much as possible, they attempt to keep their observations and conclusions objective and value-free.

➤ The first step in the scientific research process is to find a problem to investigate. After reviewing work that has already been done on a topic, the researcher poses an as-yet-unanswered question and formulates a potential answer, called a hypothesis.

➤ A hypothesis is a prediction about the relationship between two variables, one of which—the independent variable—may be manipulated to reveal changes in the other, dependent variable. Both variables must be defined in such a way that they can be measured.

➤ Sociologists collect data on research variables using questionnaires, interviews, observations, and documentary resources such as census records. Although personal interviews are a rich and reliable source of information, they are quite costly and time-consuming compared with questionnaires and telephone interviews.

➤ Besides summarizing the results of their research and drawing conclusions, sociologists must question the validity (accuracy) of their data and also decide whether their results might legitimately be applied to a broader population.

➤ There are four major types of sociological research: experiments, surveys, secondary research, and field research. Each is guided by a specific research design, or plan for collecting data.

➤ The research design for an experiment typically has four steps: (1) establish two separate groups, an experimental group and a control group; (2) assign subjects to the two groups randomly; (3) measure the dependent variable both before and after the experiments; and (4) compare the two sets of measurements.

➤ To establish a causal relationship between two variables, experimenters must satisfy four conditions: (1) the cause must occur *before* the effect; (2) the two variables must be correlated, or linked systematically; (3) the relationship between the two variables must not be explainable by some third variable; and (4) there must be a logical explanation for the presumed causal relationship.

11

➤ Sociological experiments are often performed in the field—that is, in the natural settings where people live and work. Because experimental conditions cannot be controlled in this type of setting, field experiments cannot determine causality.

➤ Surveys are a type of research well suited to studying the attitudes of large groups of people. Though surveys cannot establish a causal relationship between variables, they can quantify the relationship, and the results can often be applied to a broader population.

➤ Secondary research involves the analysis of data drawn from work of others—archives, newspapers, diaries, government statistics, or public opinion polls, for instance. This type of research is used heavily in cross-cultural studies and studies of social change.

➤ Field research usually involves the long-term, in-depth study of a group of people in their natural environment by sociologists who may choose to participate in the group. This method of research produces qualitative, or nonnumerical, data, which are generally used to develop a hypothesis about the subject under study.

➤ In the past, most sociological research was done on white, middle-class males. Guided by feminist research strategies, sociologists now study more diverse samples of people, especially women and racial minorities.

➤ Sociologists must take care to follow ethical guidelines in their research, to protect the rights and dignity of those they study. Confidentiality and informed consent—the requirement that sociologists first explain a study to participants and obtain their permission to be subjects—are imperative.

MULTIPLE CHOICE

1. Sociology is guided in its quest for knowledge by a set of standards designed to ensure that what we know is both accurate and useful. These standards are part of the _____ method.

   a. scientific
   b. empirical
   c. research
   d. generalized

2. Because there are many different options to examine before zeroing in on a final hypothesis, which stage of research is often the most difficult?

   a. building the conceptual framework
   b. reviewing the literature
   c. formulating the problem
   d. forming a hypothesis

3. By predicting an answer to the research question, the researcher is forming a hypothesis. The concepts in a hypothesis are stated as _____ – characteristics or traits that can be measured.

   a. theories
   b. conceptual frameworks
   c. paradigms
   d. variables

4. A/an _____ specifies how concepts and variables will be measured empirically.

   a. hypothesis
   b. operational definition
   c. theory
   d. paradigm

5. _____ refers to whether you are measuring what you think you are measuring.

   a. Validity
   b. Reliability
   c. Theoretical relevancy
   d. Hypothetical integrity

6. _____ refers to getting the same results if the measurement is repeated.

   a. Validity
   b. Theoretical relevancy
   c. Reliability
   d. Hypothetical integrity

7. Validity is increased through _____, the use of multiple data collection methods.

    a. reliability correlation
    b. control procedures
    c. survey control
    d. triangulation

8. In questionnaire construction, the problem with _____ is the limited choices they offer, which can make it difficult for researchers to learn all that respondents think about a subject.

    a. closed-ended questions
    b. open-ended questions
    c. mailed technique
    d. self-administration

9. Which of the following is a *disadvantage* of interviews?

    a. People would rather write than talk.
    b. Interviews are more expensive than questionnaires.
    c. Interviewer bias can creep in when a respondent needs to have a question clarified.
    d. Interviews are often invalid as a data source.

10. All stages of the research process are guided by an organized plan for collecting data, termed a/an _____ design.

    a. experimental
    b. central
    c. hypothetical
    d. research

11. In the classic experimental design, the _____ group is exposed to the independent variable.

    a. experimental
    b. control
    c. correlation
    d. spurious

12. _____ research involves using self-administered questionnaires, personal interviews, or telephone interviews to collect data about a topic of interest to the researcher.

   a. Field
   b.) Survey
   c. Qualitative
   d. Analytic

13. A _____ sample is one in which every member of the population under study had an equal chance of being chosen.

   a. stratified
   b. convenience
   c.) random
   d. secondary

14. _____ analysis relies heavily on the wealth of information available from documentary resources.

   a. Comparative
   b. Primary
   c. Random
   d.) Secondary

15. _____ analysis is a technique in which researchers systematically code and quantify the content of documents, such as magazines or newspapers, noting what they consider important to the research question.

   a.) Content
   b. Comparative
   c. Secondary
   d. Unobtrusive

16. One source of unobtrusive measures is a _____—a piece of evidence left from people's past behavior that can be examined for information about what those people valued, thought, or felt.

   a. validity symbol
   b. qualitative sign
   c. reliability indicator
   d.) physical trace

17.   _____ researchers collect data about the social behavior of people in
           natural settings.

       a.   Survey
       b.   Telephone
       c.   Field
       d.   Valid

18.   Using _____, the researcher witnesses, experiences, and engages
       firsthand in the activities of the group being studied.

       a.   field research
       b.   survey research
       c.   participant observation
       d.   mailed questionnaires

19.   In a classic study, _____ was interested in self-identity and the degree to
       which certain environments, such as prisons, could alter a person's social self.

       a.   Laud Humphreys
       b.   Philip Zimbardo
       c.   Stanley Milgram
       d.   William F. Whyte

20.   In exploring deviant behavior, _____ was interested in studying
       "tearooms"–public restrooms frequented by men in search of "instant sex" from
       other men.

       a.   Laud Humphreys
       b.   Philip Zimbardo
       c.   Stanley Milgram
       d.   William F. Whyte

TRUE-FALSE

1. F Scientific research is expected to be *subjective*, or carried out in a random
      fashion.

2. F Change in the dependent variable is presumed to cause change in the
      independent variable.

3. T Researchers can never be completely certain that measurements are accurate.

4. F Closed-ended questions ask respondents to provide their own answers to a question, rather than having to choose from a list of answers.

5. F The major advantage of the mail questionnaire is that the response rate is extremely high.

6. T Interviews eliminate some of the problems associated with self-administered questionnaires and are more flexible.

7. T Through random digit dialing, telephone numbers in desired exchanges can be randomly accessed, a procedure that permits calls to unlisted numbers, new numbers, and numbers for those who live in institutions, such as college dorms.

8. T The Hawthorne effect is most likely to occur in a field experiment in which the subjects come to the study highly motivated to "shine" in their performance.

9. F Contemporary research on social change continues to rely heavily on convenience resources to support their own theoretical approaches.

10. F Field experiments and field research are, for all practical purposes, synonymous.

ANSWERS - MULTIPLE CHOICE (correct answer/page reference)

1.	a	32
2.	c	33
3.	d	35
4.	b	36
5.	a	36
6.	c	36
7.	d	37
8.	a	37-38
9.	c	38-39
10.	d	41
11.	a	42
12.	b	44
13.	c	45
14.	d	45
15.	a	46
16.	d	47-48
17.	c	48
18.	c	49
19.	b	53-54
20.	a	54

ANSWERS - TRUE-FALSE (correct answer/page reference)

1.   F   33
2.   F   35
3.   T   37
4.   F   37
5.   F   38
6.   T   38
7.   T   40
8.   T   44
9.   F   46
10. F   48

CHAPTER 3
CULTURE

LEARNING OBJECTIVES

➢ To identify ethnocentrism and the importance of cultural relativism when studying our own and other societies.

➢ To be able to place the importance of values and beliefs in the context of the culture.

➢ To be able to see how culture distinguishes humans from other animal social groups.

➢ To learn how language helps to shape the human experience.

➢ To begin to see the processes of change in the culture.

➢ To apply the different sociological perspectives to an understanding of culture.

➢ To identify the characteristics that make a sub-culture or counter-culture.

➢ To develop an appreciation of the diversity of American culture.

CHAPTER OUTLINE

I. Culture and Society
    A. Ethnocentrism and Cultural relativism
    B. Values and Beliefs
    C. Norms and Sanctions

II. Culture as a Symbol System
    A. The Emotional Impact of Symbols
    B. Language
    C. Culturally Speaking: What Separates Humans from Other Animals

III. Cultural Change
    A. Processes of Cultural Change

IV.   Theoretical Perspectives on Culture
      A.   Functionalism
      B.   Symbolic Interaction
      C.   Conflict Theory

V.   Cultural Diversity
      A.   Subcultures: The Significance of Being Different
      B.   Counter Cultures: Different but Opposed

SUMMARY

> Culture is a shared way of life that includes everything from material objects—food, clothing, furniture—to intangibles such as life values, customs, and symbols. Culture is learned and is unique to human beings.

> Most people assume that their own culture is superior to other cultures, a view known as ethnocentrism. But sociology and anthropology are founded on the principle of cultural relativism, the presumption that all cultures must be understood and respected on their own terms.

> Values are the ideals that underlie a culture's moral standards. Americans revere the core values of individualism, achievement, and equality of opportunity, but they also value humanitarianism, a concern for those less fortunate than themselves.

> Values are expressed through rules of conduct, called norms, and penalties for violating those rules are called sanctions. Norms include both the folkways that govern daily life and the more formal mores on which a society's laws are based.

> Shared symbols, such as a flag or a language, distinguish one culture from another. Language is a key marker of a separate culture or identity; if a language is lost, the culture it represents may die with it.

> Though language does not *determine* thought, as the Sapir-Whorf hypothesis suggests, it can bias one's perceptions and behavior. The undesirable effects of negative labeling serve as one example of the power of language to bias thought.

> Language use varies with gender, based on the cultural norms and roles prescribed for men and women. American men are more assertive and less revealing in their speech than women, while women are more polite, open, and descriptive in their conversation.

- Humor is based on a shared knowledge of cultural stereotypes. While functionalists see humor as a kind of social glue, conflict theorists see jokes based on ethnic and racial slurs as masked aggression.

- Cultural integration is the incorporation of new elements into a culture, through contact with other cultures, environmental change, or innovation. Material innovations tend to be integrated more quickly than the values associated with them, creating cultural lag.

- The spread of culture from one society to another, called diffusion, can occur through direct contact between people or through the indirect exchange of goods and ideas. Cultural innovation can occur through invention—the novel use of existing cultural elements—or discovery—the creation of something entirely new.

- According to functionalist theory, all cultures share cultural universals, such as the incest taboo, religious rituals, and folklore, that aid in their survival; each culture expresses those universals in uniquely adaptive ways. But symbolic interactionists point out that not all customs are adaptive; some are downright maladaptive.

- Conflict theorists emphasize that the dominant group in a culture controls its value system and its language. Oppressed groups can use the dominant group's language to achieve their own ends, however.

- A subculture is a group whose values, norms, and mores set it apart from the mainstream culture. Subcultures may be based on race, ethnicity, religion, age, gender, occupation, sexual orientation, physical disability, or some special interest.

- A counterculture is a subculture in which the values and norms are opposed to those of the dominant culture. Student protest movements and gangs are examples of countercultures.

- Because of recent increases in immigration from Latin America, Asia, the Caribbean, Africa, and Eastern Europe, American society is becoming extremely diverse, both culturally and linguistically.

- Around the world, the trend toward globalization is threatening the survival of indigenous cultures.

MULTIPLE CHOICE

1. The text points out that *culture*

    a. is a human society's total way of life.
    b. is learned and shared.
    c. includes the society's values, customs, material objects, and symbols.
    d. all of the above

2. *Material culture* includes the

    a. values that are found in a society.
    b. traditions that are found in a society.
    c. the artifacts, physical objects, and items that are found in a society.
    d. all of the above

3. The text points out that *cultural relativism* is

    a. is synonymous with ethnocentrism.
    b. the view that all cultures have intrinsic worth and that each culture must be evaluated and understood according to its own standards.
    c. nonpragmatic.
    d. all of the above

4. _____ are cultural ideals about what is considered moral and immoral, good and bad, or proper and improper.

    a. Values
    b. Beliefs
    c. Norms
    d. Laws

5. Which one of the following is NOT an important American value?

    a. achievement
    b. material comfort
    c. nationalism
    d. group goals

6.	_____ are rules of conduct that guide people's behavior in specific situations.

    a.	Values
    b.	Beliefs
    c.	Norms
    d.	Symbols

7.	*Sanctions* are

    a.	penalties for violating norms as well as approval or reward for adhering to norms.
    b.	rules of conduct that guide people's behavior in specific situations.
    c.	norms that members of a society or culture consider vitally important, necessary, and inviolable.
    d.	cultural ideals about what is considered good and bad.

8.	*Folkways* are

    a.	rules of conduct that guide people's behavior in specific situations.
    b.	norms that members of a society or culture consider vitally important, necessary, and inviolable.
    c.	cultural ideals about what is considered good and bad.
    d.	informal norms governing customary ways of behaving.

9.	A/an _____ is something that stands for or represents something else and is given meaning by those who use it.

    a.	norm
    b.	symbol
    c.	value
    d.	belief

10.	"Different languages have different grammars and vocabulary, and these in turn affect what people notice, label, and think about as well as how they organize and categorize what they perceive." This describes the

    a.	psychoanalytic approach.
    b.	environmental perspective.
    c.	Sapir-Whorf hypothesis.
    d.	sociocultural approach.

11. According to research on language and gender,

    a. men use more qualifiers and tag questions than women.
    b. women use less polite speech and more direct forms of address than men.
    c. men converse in open, free-flowing ways and appreciate self-disclosure.
    d. none of the above

12. _____ describes the process by which cultural elements become connected and mutually interdependent.

    a. Diffusion
    b. Cultural integration
    c. Cultural lag
    d. Ethnocentrism

13. Because different parts of the culture change at different rates, a gap often exists between the time an artifact is introduced and the time it is integrated into a culture's value system. This gap is an example of cultural

    a. lag.
    b. diffusion.
    c. integration.
    d. ethnocentrism.

14. The spread of cultural elements, both material and nonmaterial, from one society to another is called

    a. cultural integration.
    b. cultural lag.
    c. diffusion.
    d. ethnocentrism.

15. Cultural change occurs through _____, when existing cultural elements are combined to create new ones.

    a. invention
    b. discovery
    c. alteration
    d. commonality

16.   Cultural change occurs through _____ when new cultural elements are created or existing cultural elements are reinterpreted.

        a. commonality
        b. invention
        c. alteration
        d. discovery

17.   All known prehistoric and historic societies are thought to have common features, called _____, that aided in their survival.

        a. universal norms
        b. cultural universals
        c. descriptive features
        d. inventive characteristics

18.   According to the functionalist perspective, unique customs develop and persist because they are

        a. universal.
        b. prescriptive.
        c. adaptive.
        d. relational.

19.   A _____ is a variation on mainstream culture, a group whose values and norms, folkways and mores set them apart from the broader culture.

        a. subculture
        b. counterculture
        c. contraculture
        d. biculture

20.   Sometimes the distinctiveness of a subculture puts it in such sharp contrast with the broader culture that it becomes a _____, with values and norms in opposition to the dominant culture.

        a. biculture
        b. ethnoculture
        c. contraculture
        d. counterculture

TRUE-FALSE

1. T For social scientists or those who simply want to study or comprehend another culture, ethnocentrism is dysfunctional.

2. T In small, traditional, relatively isolated societies, agreement on values may be close to universal.

3. F *Mores* are informal norms governing customary ways of behaving.

4. T All cultures are represented through language.

5. F In American culture, *personal distance* extends to about 18 inches.

6. T A recent study showed that people are thirty times more likely to laugh when it groups than when alone.

7. T Most nonhuman animals communicate.

8. F Multiculturalism has a singular level of meaning.

9. F Ethnocide refers to the annihilation of an ethnic group.

10. F Deliberate ethnocide is rare today because of global consensus on human rights.

ANSWERS - MULTIPLE CHOICE   (correct answer/page reference)

1.	d	59
2.	c	60
3.	b	61
4.	a	61
5.	d	62
6.	c	64
7.	a	64
8.	d	64
9.	b	64
10.	c	65
11.	d	68
12.	b	71
13.	a	71
14.	c	71

15.	a	72
16.	d	72
17.	b	72
18.	c	73
19.	a	76
20.	d	76

ANSWERS - TRUE-FALSE (correct answer/page reference)

1.	T	61
2.	T	61
3.	F	64
4.	T	65
5.	F	67
6.	T	68
7.	T	70
8.	F	78
9.	F	80
10.	F	81

CHAPTER 4
SOCIAL STRUCTURE

LEARNING OBJECTIVES

➤ To be able to identify status, master status, and status set, and show how these contribute to the social structure.

➤ To learn how roles provide a script for occupants of a given social position and how role conflict and strain may be resolved.

➤ To be able to distinguish between secondary and primary groups and how the relative numbers of secondary and primary relationships have altered with the growth and change of society.

➤ To identify the connections among the interpretations of societal change of Durkheim, Tönnies and the Lenskis, and the importance of these interpretations of social evolution.

➤ To be able to place the elements of social structure—networks, formal organizations, communities, strata, institutions and societies—in relation to one another.

➤ To be able to apply the concepts of structure to the continuing change in social structure.

CHAPTER OUTLINE

I. Status and Role
    A. Status
    B. Role

II. Social Groups
    A. Types of Groups
    B. Group Dynamics

III. Larger elements of Social Structure
    A. Networks
    B. Formal Organizations
    C. Communities
    D. Strata
    E. Institutions
    F. Societies

SUMMARY

- Social structure consists of the relatively stable patterns of social interaction that characterize human social life; it is within the context of social structure that people enact culture.

- Statuses are the key components from which larger units of social structure are constructed.

- Statuses may be ascribed or achieved; when a status is especially important in determining an individual's identity, it is called a master status.

- Roles are the dynamic aspect of statuses—we occupy a status but play a role.

- Role strain and role conflict can result when people play several roles at the same time.

- Social groups consist of several people who regularly interact and feel some sense of solidarity or common identity.

- Primary groups provide warmth and intimacy, whereas secondary groups are important for accomplishing specific objectives.

- In-groups, out-groups, and reference groups are other important types of social groups.

- The size of a group is crucial in determining how it functions.

- All groups have two types of leaders: instrumental leaders, who concentrate on achieving group goals, and expressive leaders, who maintain group morale.

- People in small groups feel strong pressure to conform to the expectations of others and to obey group leaders.

- Groupthink can interfere with the ability of a cohesive group to make wise decisions.

- Networks are an increasingly important type of relatively diffuse social structure.

- Larger elements of social structure include formal organizations, communities, strata, institutions, and societies.

➢ Durkheim identified an historical transition from mechanical to organic solidarity; Tönnies analyzed the same shift using the term *Gemeinschaft* and *Gesellschaft*.

➢ Gerhard and Jean Lenski argue that sociohistorical evolution proceeds through several stages: hunting and gathering, horticultural or pastoral, agrarian, industrial, and postindustrial.

➢ In the future, social structure is likely to become more diffuse and more global.

MULTIPLE CHOICE

1. A ten-year old college student or a Ph.D. working behind the counter of a fast food restaurant are both examples of

    a. normative dissensus.
    b. status inconsistency.
    c. ascribed statuses.
    d. anomie.

2. Sociologically, _____ may denote prestigious positions or those that others look down upon.

    a. cultural norms
    b. a status set
    c. status symbols
    d. achieved statuses

3. Which of the following is NOT an ascribed status?

    a. occupation
    b. gender
    c. race
    d. ethnicity

4. Which of the following is NOT an achieved status?

    a. occupation
    b. educational level
    c. political affiliation
    d. gender

5. Social positions like president of the United States, a priest, and being convicted of a capital crime, all represent _____ statuses.

    a. ascribed
    b. master
    c. conflicting
    d. secondary

6. Master statuses may be negative, in which case they are called

    a. social blemishes.
    b. tokens.
    c. stigmas.
    d. status sets.

7. _____ are the norms associated with a status; they define the behaviors expected of an individual occupying that particular status.

    a. Roles
    b. Stigmas
    c. Status symbols
    d. Status sets

8. Most important statuses are accompanied by a cluster of related but somewhat distinct roles or what may be called

    a. role conflict.
    b. a role set.
    c. role reversal.
    d. role destination.

9. Sometimes people experience role _____ – difficulty performing all the elements of the role set connected to a single status.

    a. conflict
    b. overload
    c. strain
    d. reversal

10. A sociologists use the term, a _____ consists of two or more people who regularly interact and feel some sense of solidarity or common identity.

    a. role embracement
    b. role set
    c. compartmentalization
    d. social group

11. Charles Horton Cooley used the term _____ to refer to small groups characterized by warm, informal, and long-lasting interaction.

    a. secondary group
    b. primary group
    c. looking-glass self
    d. categories

12. _____ groups tend to be formal, emotionally cool, and are often temporary.

    a. Secondary
    b. Primary
    c. Categorical
    d. Social

13. When traveling in Europe, everyone from the United States is part of a/an _____ group.

    a. colloquial
    b. reference
    c. in-
    d. out-

14. Someone from Texas may well view a New Yorker as a member of a/an

    a. in-
    b. uncolloquial
    c. anti-reference
    d. out-

15. _____ groups are composed of people we look to in order to evaluate our own behavior.

   a. Reference
   b. In-
   c. Out-
   d. Colloquial

16. Irving Janis identified a phenomenon called _____ that refers to the tendency of highly cohesive groups to make poor decisions because the members are unwilling to threaten the group's solidarity.

   a. anomic decision making
   b. groupthink
   c. collective thinking
   d. relational thinking

17. Durkheim argued that most societies throughout history have been characterized by high levels of

   a. anomie.
   b. organic solidarity.
   c. mechanical solidarity.
   d. *Gesellschaft.*

18. Durkheim argued that as societies grow, a new type of social bond emerges, called _____, which is based not on similarity but rather on difference and interdependence.

   a. organic solidarity
   b. *Gemeinschaft*
   c. mechanical solidarity
   d. anomie

19. Ferdinand Tönnies called a society constructed primarily on the basis of natural will relationships a/an

   a. anomic state.
   b. *Gesellschaft.*
   c. organic state.
   d. *Gemeinschaft.*

20. Ferdinand Tönnies used the word _____ to designate a society based largely on rational will.

   (a.) *Gesellschaft*
   b. *Gemeinschaft*
   c. organic solidarity
   d. mechanical solidarity

TRUE-FALSE

1. F The sociological use of the word *status* is identical to everyday usage.

2. T Role overload takes place when there is just not enough time to perform all of one's roles properly.

3. F Role strain and role conflict are synonymous.

4. F Dyads are three-person groups.

5. F Instrumental leaders are socioemotional leaders.

6. F A laissez-faire leader is highly directive, encouraging members to make decisions with other people's help.

7. T Networks are person-specific; that is, they are different for each individual.

8. T Social classes, castes, genders, racial and ethnic groups, and different age categories are all examples of *strata*.

9. F Horticulturalists raise domesticated animals.

10. F Advanced industrial societies are rapidly moving toward a *postindustrial* model, where the economy is based more on manufacturing than services.

ANSWERS - MULTIPLE CHOICE (correct answer/page reference)

1.	b	87
2.	c	87
3.	a	87
4.	d	88
5.	b	88
6.	c	88
7.	a	88
8.	b	88
9.	c	89
10.	d	90
11.	b	91
12.	a	92
13.	c	93
14.	d	93
15.	a	93
16.	b	98
17.	c	100
18.	a	101
19.	d	101
20.	a	102

ANSWERS - TRUE-FALSE (correct answer/page reference)

1.	F	87
2.	T	89
3.	F	89
4.	F	94
5.	F	95
6.	F	96
7.	T	98
8.	T	99
9.	F	104
10.	F	107

CHAPTER 5
SOCIALIZATION

LEARNING OBJECTIVES

➢ To be able to identify the differences between nature and nurture as sources of human behavior.

➢ To learn the sociobiological arguments for human behavior.

➢ To relate gender socialization to the different theories of personality and social development.

➢ To understand the stages in cognitive and moral development.

➢ To be able to identify the elements of the life course view of socialization.

➢ To be able to identify the agents of socialization and state their importance in the development of self.

CHAPTER OUTLINE

I.   Theoretical Perspectives on Socialization
      A.   Sociobiology: Nature versus Nurture
      B.   Sociology: Symbolic Interaction and the Development of the Self
      C.   Psychology: Socialization in Crisis

II.   Socialization and the Life Course: Linking Sociology and Psychology
      A.   Psychosocial Behavior
      B.   The Sociology of Adult Development and Aging
      C.   The Life Course: A Critical Review

III. Nature and Nurture: The Debate Resolved

SUMMARY

➢ Socialization is the lifelong process through which individuals acquire culture, develop their sense of self, and become functioning members of society.

➢ Sociobiologists believe that human behavior is determined genetically, according to evolutionary principles. Not much evidence exists for this view.

- Symbolic interactionists stress the importance of role-playing and the looking-glass-self—imagining what others think of us—in developing social identity.

- According to Freud, socialization is a multistage process in which the child struggles to reconcile basic biological drives with conflicting social norms and values. This highly influential theory is essentially untestable.

- Social learning theorists hold that children are socialized both indirectly, through observation and imitation of others, and directly, through rewards and punishments for specific behaviors.

- Jean Piaget, a cognitive theorist, proposed a multistage theory of cognitive development that became the foundation for several studies of moral development. Best known are Lawrence Kohlberg's work, which suggested that boys reach a higher stage of moral development than girls, and Carol Gilligan's follow-up study, which indicated that girls use different but equally valid norms in their moral reasoning.

- The life course perspective on socialization is an interdisciplinary approach that stresses adult as well as child development. Life course theorists are particularly interested in the defining attitudes and behaviors of birth cohorts, those who age together and experience events in history as a generation.

- Eric Erickson proposed that humans develop through eight life stages, each marked by special challenges and a central developmental crisis.

- Research shows that in early and middle adulthood married couples juggle multiple responsibilities, testing the strength of their relationships as they attempt to resolve conflict between career and family.

- Compared with early and middle adulthood, later adulthood and old age are a time of role loss, although new roles may be substituted. As physical strength diminishes, activity level drops and the elderly begin to look back in time rather than forward.

- Elisabeth Kubler-Ross identified five stages people go through in coming to terms with death. Research suggests, however, that the dying do not necessarily progress through those stages in a set sequence.

- Though many sociologists associate certain life activities and gender role norms with specific ages, life course theories do not apply to all people and all cultures. In the United States, social change has altered the age at which many adults marry, have children, and enter and leave the labor force.

➤ The family is the primary agent of socialization especially in the first years of life, nurturing self-esteem, providing language learning and cognitive development, and conferring social status (class, race, ethnicity, and religion) on the child.

➤ In later childhood, the schools become influential social agents, teaching social skills and communicating core cultural values and gender role expectations to students. Gender-segregated peer groups formed at school are another means of socialization during these years.

➤ The mass media, especially television, may socialize young viewers in a negative way through their portrayal of violence and gender stereotyped role models.

➤ Resocialization, a process designed to eliminate destructive behaviors or alter behavior to fit new goals, is often pursued in institutions that exert control over people's lives, such as prisons. Rather than rehabilitate criminals, however, most prisons in the United States reinforce inmates' destructive behavior patterns.

MULTIPLE CHOICE

1. _____ is the lifelong process whereby we learn our culture, develop our sense of self, and become functioning members of society.

    a. Psychological development
    b. Psychosocial maturation
    c. Socialization
    d. Social maturity

2. Which field addresses the similarities and differences between humans and lower animals by examining the biological roots of social behavior?

    a. sociology
    b. psychology
    c. social psychology
    d. sociobiology

3.   What is the unique sense of identity, agreed upon by both sociologists and psychologists, that distinguishes each individual from all other individuals?

   a.   personality
   b.   self
   c.   ego
   d.   id

4.   _____ is the distinctive complex of attitudes, beliefs, behaviors, and values that make up an individual.

   a.   Self
   b.   Ego
   c.   Personality
   d.   Superego

5.   Sociologist Charles Horton Cooley maintained that we imagine how others see us and we imagine their judgment of that appearance; our image of ourselves then develops based on that imagination. Cooley referred to this process as the

   a.   looking-glass self.
   b.   superego.
   c.   "I" and the "me."
   d.   personality formation.

6.   Those people whose approval and affection we desire the most and who are therefore most important to the development of our self-concept are called

   a.   alter egos.
   b.   personality types.
   c.   significant others.
   d.   the generalized other.

7.   We imagine what others think of us and we also imagine what it is like to be in their shoes. The latter process is referred to as

   a.   primary socialization.
   b.   secondary socialization.
   c.   the generalized other.
   d.   role-taking.

8. By age twelve most children have developed an awareness of the _____: the ability to understand broader cultural norms and judge what a typical person might think or do.

   a. significant other
   b. generalized other
   c. superego
   d. id

9. During the early years of life, _____ socialization occurs, during which language is learned and the first sense of self is gained.

   a. primary
   b. secondary
   c. initial
   d. subsequent

10. George is a freshman in college and aspires to become a member of a fraternity. He begins to behave in accordance with how he believes a "fraternity man" should act. This illustrates which type of socialization?

    a. primary
    b. secondary
    c. anticipatory
    d. resocialization

11. The _____ is Freud's term for an individual's biological drives and impulses—selfish, irrational, unconscious, and ever-striving for pleasure and gratification.

    a. superego
    b. id
    c. ego
    d. Oedipus complex

12. The _____ is Freud's term for all the norms, values, and morals that are learned through socialization.

    a. Electra complex
    b. id
    c. ego
    d. superego

13. According to Freudian theory, the _____ acts as a mediator between the biological drives and the society that would deny them.

 a. ego
 b. superego
 c. id
 d. subconscious

14. According to _____ theory, once the child learns cultural definitions of gender, these definitions become the core around which all other information is organized.

 a. functional
 b. conflict
 c. gender schema
 d. interactionist

15. Unlike other phases of adulthood, transition to old age is often noted by a retirement dinner, a gold watch, or a special birthday celebration. These events constitute

 a. formal rites of passage.
 b. anticipatory socialization.
 c. geriatric socialization.
 d. informal designs.

16. The people, groups, and social institutions that provide the critical information needed for children to become fully functioning members of society are referred to as

 a. the generalized other.
 b. agents of socialization.
 c. significant others.
 d. superegos.

17. Besides the formal academic agenda, schools also have a powerful _____, which includes all the informal, unwritten norms that exist both inside and outside the classroom.

 a. philosophical undercurrent
 b. stereotype
 c. cultural bias
 d. hidden curriculum

18. _____ are made up of people who are the same age and generally share the same interests and positions.

    a. Peer groups
    b. Informal associations
    c. Formal groups
    d. Reference groups

19. When socialization fails, most people must go through the process of _____ in order to remedy patterns of behavior that society finds destructive or to alter behavior to make it fit with other personal or social goals.

    a. psychological renewal
    b. resocialization
    c. rehabilitation
    d. sociological rebirth

20. Erving Goffman has written about places of residence and work that exert complete control over the people they contain. Goffman referred to these locations as

    a. total institutions.
    b. rehabilitative associations.
    c. *Gemeinschaft*.
    d. *Gesellschaft*.

TRUE-FALSE

1. F Gender socialization is the process by which individuals learn how to play their biological roles in reproduction.

2. F According to George Herbert Mead, the *game stage* of socialization occurs from birth to about age three.

3. T Of Freud's five stages of psychosexual development, the one that has received the most attention is the *phallic* stage.

4. T Once we develop our gender identity, we perceive ourselves as either male or female.

5. F According to Piaget, the capacity for abstract reasoning (the formal operational stage) develops at around age six.

6. f The *life course* perspective of socialization underscores the fundamental schism between sociology and psychology.

7. T Erik Erikson proposed eight "psychosocial" stages that all people must go through from infancy to old age.

8. T Research shows that the *empty nest syndrome* is largely a myth.

9. f The first stage in Kübler-Ross's "death course" is *bargaining*.

10. T Television is by far the most influential of the media.

ANSWERS - MULTIPLE CHOICE (correct answer/page reference)

1.	c	114
2.	d	115
3.	b	115
4.	c	115
5.	a	116
6.	c	117
7.	d	117
8.	b	117
9.	a	117
10.	c	117
11.	b	118
12.	d	118
13.	a	118
14.	c	123
15.	a	129
16.	b	133
17.	d	134
18.	a	135
19.	b	137
20.	a	138

ANSWERS - TRUE-FALSE (correct answer/page reference)

1. F 114
2. F 117
3. T 119
4. T 120
5. F 122
6. F 124
7. T 125
8. T 128
9. F 130-131
10. T 136

CHAPTER 6
SOCIAL INTERACTION: CONSTRUCTING THE MEANING OF EVERYDAY LIFE

LEARNING OBJECTIVES

➤ To learn how the creation of social reality affects what is presumed to be a completely biological characteristic of human behavior.

➤ To be able to identify how perception creates a definition of the situation.

➤ To understand the importance of impression management in the performance of our roles.

➤ To be able to distinguish between role expectations and role performance.

➤ To be able to explain how differences in gender roles have nearly disappeared.

➤ To be able to identify the nature of non-verbal communication as it relates to gender roles.

➤ To be able to show how social construction of child abuse, poverty and environmental degradation transforms these to social problems.

CHAPTER OUTLINE

I. The Social Construction of Reality
   A. Symbolic Interaction
   B. Ethnomethodology
   C. Life-as-Theater
   D. Impression Management
   E. Critiquing the Social Construction of Reality

II. Human Sexuality
   A. Sexuality in a Diverse World
   B. Gender Identity and Sexual Orientation
   C. Gender Differences in Sexuality
   D. Sexuality in Later Life
   E. Sexuality as Socially Constructed

III. Nonverbal Communication
   A. Nonverbal Communication as a Polygraph
   B. Cultural Variations in Nonverbal Communication

SUMMARY

➤ Social interaction is an active, dynamic process in which participants may choose from a range of socially accepted behaviors. In doing so, people construct their own reality and modify existing cultural norms.

➤ According to symbolic interaction theory, people interact on the basis of their own perceptions of a situation, and their assumptions about others' perceptions.

➤ Ethnomethodology is the study of the taken-for-granted-rules that govern social interactions.

➤ According to Erving Goffman's dramaturgical approach, social interactions are similar to theatrical performances, and are culturally and socially prescribed. People play the roles conferred on them by their social status.

➤ Symbolic interactionists hold that people try to manage the impressions they give others to protect their self-esteem and to please others.

➤ According to symbolic interactionists, gender identity and sexual orientation are socially constructed, which accounts for the great diversity in human sexual expression. Gender roles, sexual orientation, and the concept of beauty differ markedly from one culture to the next.

➤ Studies of hermaphrodites—people whose biological sex is ambiguous—lend support to the theory that gender is socially constructed. Depending on whether they are raised as girls or boys, hermaphrodites can develop a female or male gender identity.

➤ Surveys of Americans' sexual behavior shows that over the last half-century, gender differences in sexual behavior have virtually disappeared. But men and women still hold different attitudes toward sexual expression: women are more cautious and deliberate in their choice of partners than men. Women are also judged more negatively than men when they engage in nonmarital sex.

➤ Research done by Masters and Johnson shows that negative labeling can create self-fulfilling prophecies that discourage sexual expression, especially among women and the elderly.

➤ Like sexual expression, nonverbal communication—gestures, facial expressions, eye contact, touching, tone of voice, speed and volume of speech—is socially constructed; it differs widely from one culture to the next.

➤ Studies of Americans have revealed gender differences in the use of nonverbal communication. These differences are rooted in gender subcultures and the unequal social status of men and women.

➤ Functionalists suggest that gender differences in nonverbal communication help to maintain social equilibrium by reinforcing differences in gender roles. But conflict theorists see such differences as evidence of the differences in power between men and women.

➤ According to symbolic interactionists, social problems like poverty, child abuse, and environmental degradation are socially constructed. Only when they are defined as social threats by large numbers of people do they become problems.

➤ Sexual harassment has been redefined as a social problem, but because there is disagreement about what it constitutes, there is ambivalence about policies to deal with it.

MULTIPLE CHOICE

1. How people behave toward one another when they meet is referred to as

   a. psychological contact.
   b. social interaction.
   c. human interchange.
   d. psychosocial relationships.

2. The ways in which we perceive and express ourselves as sexual beings is referred to as

   a. human sexuality.
   b. psychosexual interaction.
   c. bisexual relationship.
   d. microlevel sexuality.

3. When sociologists examine social interaction from a *microlevel* perspective they concentrate on the

   a. global backdrop of interaction dynamics.
   b. "big picture."
   c. details of interaction that usually occur between two people or in other small groups.
   d. both a and b above

4. How do people socially construct their everyday world and give meaning to their experiences and interactions? _____ seeks to answer this question by understanding social interaction from the person's own frame of reference.

    a. Social exchange theory
    b. Functionalism
    c. Conflict theory
    d. Ethnomethodology

5. Erving Goffman views social interaction as a play being acted out on a stage. Goffman's perspective is referred to as the _____ approach.

    a. psychosocial
    b. dramaturgical
    c. psychosexual
    d. developmental

6. The dramaturgical approach to social interaction in everyday life is expanded by Goffman through his model of _____–all the "small behaviors" that make up encounters, such as glances, gestures, positionings, and verbal statements.

    a. frontstage behavior
    b. backstage behavior
    c. interaction ritual
    d. anomie assessment

7. In social encounters we use strategies of _____ to provide information, usually in the form of subtle and not so subtle cues, to present ourselves in the best possible light.

    a. frontstage behavior
    b. impression management
    c. backstage behavior
    d. interaction ritual

8. Students who usually come to class in tattered jeans and t-shirts will put on "nicer" cloths for a class presentation. According to Erving Goffman, this represents _____ behavior.

    a. frontstage
    b. backstage
    c. stage left
    d. stage right

9. If you believe you lack self-confidence, it in turn increases the risk that the person you are asking out will decline the offer. In this instance, _____ is a likely diagnosis.

    a. a personality disorder
    b. a psychosocial complaint
    c. anomie
    d. a self-fulfilling prophecy

10. A person's preference for sexual partners is termed

    a. sexual orientation.
    b. gender identity.
    c. gender orientation.
    d. gender roles.

11. _____ refers to those biological characteristics distinguishing male and female.

    a. Gender
    b. Sex
    c. Dimorphism
    d. Berdache

12. _____ refers to those social, cultural and psychological characteristics linked to male and female that define people as masculine and feminine.

    a. Xanith
    b. Dimorphism
    c. Gender
    d. Sex

13. The separation of the sexes into two distinct groups reflects the principle of

    a. gender distinctiveness.
    b. sexual dimorphism.
    c. gender identity.
    d. sexual segregation.

14. *Anorexia nervosa* is a disease

    a. that primarily affects males.
    b. involving the digestive system.
    c. of the stomach.
    d. of self-induced weight loss, primarily affecting young women.

15. Children born with both male and female sexual organs or ambiguous genitals are referred to as

    a. hermaphrodites.
    b. transvestites.
    c. transsexuals.
    d. bisexuals.

16. _____ are genetic males or females who undergo sex reassignment surgery.

    a. Hermaphrodites
    b. Transvestites
    c. Transsexuals
    d. Bisexuals

17. Body movements such as gestures, facial expressions, eye contact, use of personal space, and touching are all examples of

    a. socialization dynamics.
    b. nonverbal communication.
    c. psychological dynamics.
    d. cultural components.

18. According to research on gender differences in communication, women

    a. interrupt men more than men interrupt women.
    b. engage in less eye-contact than men.
    c. are more talkative than men in mixed-gender groups.
    d. none of the above

19. According to the Equal Employment Opportunity Commission, "unwelcome sexual advances, requests for sexual favors, and other verbal or physical conduct of a sexual nature" constitute

    a. sexual harassment.
    b. rape.
    c. sexual assault.
    d. all of the above

20. The subordination of women that is embedded in social institutions is termed

    a. sexual discrimination.
    b. sexual harassment.
    c. institutionalized sexism.
    d. gender bias.

TRUE-FALSE

1. F "Backstage" behavior is performed in a manner others expect.

2. F Sociologists who adopt the symbolic interactionist approach use a *macrolevel* perspective.

3. F In some Native American tribes, the title of *berdache* is conferred on homosexual males.

4. T *Bisexuals* have shifting sexual orientations and are sexually responsive to either sex.

5. T Negative labeling can create self-fulfilling prophecies that discourage pleasurable sex for women and any sex for the elderly.

6. F The text concludes that the disappearance of a sexual double standard is extremely desirable.

7. T Too much discrepancy between verbal and nonverbal language can generate mistrust and suspicion.

8. F When emotions are masked completely, *leakage* always occurs.

9. T According to research on gender differences in communication, even when men speak two to three times longer than women, the men believe they do not have their fair share of communication.

10. T Symbolic interactionists explain that social issues arise through a process of collective definition.

ANSWERS - MULTIPLE CHOICE (correct answer/page reference)

1.	b	144
2.	a	144
3.	c	144
4.	d	146
5.	b	147
6.	c	148
7.	b	149
8.	a	150
9.	d	150
10.	a	151
11.	b	153
12.	c	153
13.	b	153
14.	d	153
15.	a	155
16.	c	156
17.	b	160
18.	d	161-162
19.	a	164
20.	c	165

ANSWERS - TRUE-FALSE (correct answer/page reference)

1.	F	150
2.	F	151
3.	F	153
4.	T	156
5.	T	159
6.	F	159
7.	T	160
8.	F	160
9.	T	162
10.	T	163

CHAPTER 7
COLLECTIVE BEHAVIOR AND SOCIAL MOVEMENTS

LEARNING OBJECTIVES

➢ To understand why deviance is relative.

➢ To be able to identify the way deviance is defined and who actually defines deviance.

➢ To be able to identify the role that social control plays in the community.

➢ To be able to distinguish among the biological, psychological and sociological explanations of deviance.

➢ To relate the structural strain and lower-class focal value theories to control of deviance.

➢ To identify how labeling helps to keep people deviant.

➢ To understand how behaviors have changed from deviant to non-deviant and sometimes back again.

CHAPTER OUTLINE

I.   What is Deviance?
        A. The Nature of Deviance
        B. Deviance and Social Control

II.   Four Questions About Deviance

III.   Who Defines What is Deviant?

IV   What are the Functions of Deviance?

V.   Why Do People Deviate:
        A. Biological Positivism
        B. Psychological Positivism
        C. Sociological Positivism

VII.   Social Reaction to Deviance

SUMMARY

- Sociologists consider deviance a relative concept; therefore no behavior is seen as inherently deviant. Deviance is found in all societies.

- Deviance may be interpreted as a negative label established and applied by the socially powerful. Actions, beliefs, and conditions may all be labeled deviant.

- Social control is intended to encourage conformity and discourage deviance. It may consist of either punishments or rewards. Social control may be exercised by formal or informal agents and is also a consequence of moral socialization.

- Conflict theory emphasizes the ability of social elites to define what is regarded as deviant in line with their own interests.

- Although deviance makes social life problematic, erodes trust, and is very costly to control, it also serves several positive functions. It sets the boundaries of what is regarded as acceptable behavior, encourages solidarity, and warns that change is needed.

- Biological and psychological positivism explain the origins of deviance in terms of internal factors; sociological positivism emphasizes the importance of external factors located in the social environment.

- Social structure theories, such as Merton's strain theory or Miller's lower-class focal value theory, explain the high rates of deviance among the poor and minorities by reference to broad structural factors such as blocked opportunity or distinctive subcultural values.

- Social process theories, such as Sutherland's differential association theory or Hirschi's control theory, explain individual decisions to deviate by references to factors such as social learning or bonds to conventional society.

- Labeling theory explores the consequences of applying deviant labels to individuals. It assumes that stigma is likely to become a self-fulfilling prophecy.

- In modern societies, which are characterized by considerable normative ambiguity, many forms of behavior once considered severely deviant and repressed come to be redefined as illness rather than sin. In some cases, these behaviors are later further reinterpreted as nondeviant and hence worthy of acceptance.

- However, sometimes the repression-medicalization-acceptance cycle reverses, and previously accepted behaviors such as drunk driving or tobacco smoking come to be seen as deviant.

MULTIPLE CHOICE

1. _____ is a violation of a formal statute enacted by a legitimate government.

   a. Deviance
   b. Crime
   c. Malfeasance
   d. Immorality

2. Sociologists use the term _____ in referring to any measures taken by members of society which are intended to ensure conformity to norms.

   a. social control
   b. negative sanctions
   c. positive sanctions
   d. rehabilitation

3. _____ consist(s) of efforts to discourage deviance made by people such as police officers and college deans whose jobs involve, in whole or in part, punishing nonconformity and rewarding obedience.

   a. Negative sanctions
   b. Informal social control
   c. Formal social control
   d. Positive sanctions

4. Punishments, referred to as _____, are especially important at the formal level.

   a. formal social control
   b. negative sanctions
   c. informal social control
   d. torts

5. Formal social control may involve _____ or rewards, such as a good conduct medal or an "A" on an examination.

   a. perks
   b. enhancements
   c. inducements
   d. positive sanctions

6. An extremely effective way to reduce deviance is through positive and negative sanctions applied by family and friends, referred to as

   a. normative internalization.
   b. informal social control.
   c. formal social control.
   d. shunning.

7. Enlightenment thinkers such as Caesare Beccaria and Jeremy Bentham asserted that deviance could best be understood as a consequence of exercise of free will. This perspective is known as

   a. classical theory.
   b. positivism.
   c. Sociopathy.
   d. Sociobiology.

8. Over the past two decades, the point of view that deviants consciously assess the costs and benefits of conformity and nonconformity and choose the latter only when it seems advantageous to do so, has enjoyed renewed popularity. This perspective has been referred to as

   a. positivism.
   b. sociopathy.
   c. rational choice theory.
   d. sociobiology.

9. _____ is an approach to understanding human behavior based on the scientific method.

   a. Classical theory
   b. Sociobiology
   c. Rational choice theory
   d. Positivism

10. Serial killers are usually diagnosed as _____ –individuals with high antisocial personalities lacking any appreciable conscience.

    a. paranoid schizophrenics
    b. manic depressives
    c. sociopaths
    d. anomic

11. Robert Merton used the term _____ in describing people trapped in a blocked opportunity situation, who drop out and stop seeking any goals beyond immediate self-indulgence.

a) retreatist
b. rebel
c. innovator
d. ritualist

12. Grounded in the _____ paradigm, the labeling perspective explores how the label of "deviant" is applied to particular people and the ways in which this devalued identity influences their subsequent behavior.

a. functionalist
b.) interactionist
c. conflict
d. developmental

13. The purpose of labeling is to apply a/an _____–a powerfully negative public identity to an individual who is believed to have violated important group norms.

a.) stigma
b. normative indicator
c. anomic tag
d. deviant role

14. Criminal trials, sanity hearings, and court martials are all examples of

a. secondary deviance.
b. primary deviance.
c. career deviance.
d.) degradation ceremonies.

15. _____ deviance refers to any deviant act that is *not* followed by some form of labeling.

a. Secondary
b. Career
c.) Primary
d. Relative

16. That period of time in which a person is compelled to reorganize one's life around a devalued identity is referred to as _____ deviance.

    a. primary
    b. secondary
    c. relative
    d. tertiary

17. Consider this statement: "Last week, George feel asleep in class; I thought he was just tired but now that I know he's an addict, I realize he was high." This illustrates

    a. retrospective reinterpretation.
    b. primary deviance.
    c. backstage behavior.
    d. impression management.

18. If one accepts the labeling perspective, it leads to the conclusion that in order to avoid role engulfment, we should minimize the number of people who are publicly labeled. This reflects a policy termed

    a. primary deviance.
    b. secondary deviance.
    c. retrospective reinterpretation.
    d. radical nonintervention.

19. _____ deviance involves a redefinition of the character of the deviant from "evil" to "sick."

    a. Primary
    b. Secondary
    c. The medicalization of
    d. Tertiary

20. Some organized groups of deviants have campaigned for redefinition: from medicalization to *acceptance*. John Kitsuse calls such group efforts to achieve acceptance

    a. the antimedicalization of deviance.
    b. radical intervention.
    c. retrospective reinterpretation.
    d. tertiary deviance.

TRUE-FALSE

1. F The text defines deviance as behavior that violates existing laws.

2. T From a sociological perspective, deviance is *relative*.

3. T Deviance is a cultural universal.

4. F Formal social control is society's main line of defense against deviance.

5. F In William Chambliss's study of two groups of juveniles, the "Roughnecks" were generally perceived as the *good* boys.

6. T Conflict theory's great strength is that it directs our attention to the importance of power in shaping societal definitions of deviance.

7. T When any type of deviance becomes more common, it sends a signal that something is wrong in society.

8. F Research strongly suggests some linkage between genetics and deviance and this means that a significant amount of violent crime is caused exclusively by physiological factors.

9. T Based on the work of Sigmund Freud, the *psychoanalytic* approach holds that criminals typically suffer from weak or damaged egos or from inadequate superegos that are unable to restrain the aggressive and often antisocial drives of the id.

10. F According to differential association theory, deviance is inherited, not learned.

ANSWERS - MULTIPLE CHOICE (correct answer/page reference)

1.	b	170
2.	a	172-173
3.	c	173
4.	b	173
5.	d	173
6.	b	173
7.	a	179
8.	c	179
9.	d	179
10.	c	181
11.	a	183
12.	b	186
13.	a	186
14.	d	187
15.	c	187
16.	b	187
17.	a	188
18.	d	189
19.	c	192
20.	d	193

ANSWERS - TRUE-FALSE (correct answer/page reference)

1.	F	170
2.	T	170
3.	T	172
4.	F	173
5.	F	174
6.	T	176
7.	T	177
8.	F	180
9.	T	181
10.	F	185

CHAPTER 8
CRIME AND CRIMINAL JUSTICE

LEARNING OBJECTIVES

➢   To be able to distinguish among the three broad families of criminal law.

➢   To be aware of the quality of crime statistics and how these relate to victimization.

➢   To be able to show how the United States compares to other countries with regard to criminal rates.

➢   To be able to identify the major types of crime, and place them in relationship to one another.

➢   To understand how the criminal justice system works and what the purposes of punishment are.

➢   To be able to relate the numbers who commit crimes to the people against whom the crimes are committed.

➢   To begin to identify the main points of the debate about capital punishment and the decriminalization of drug use.

CHAPTER OUTLINE

I.   Crime and the Criminal Law
    A.   Three families of Criminal Law

II.   Crime Rates
    A.   Measuring Crime
    B.   Crime Rates in the United States
    C.   Crime Rates in Cross-Cultural Perspective

III.   Major Types of Crime
    A.   Violent Street Crime
    B.   Elite Crime
    C.   Victimless Crime

IV.   The Criminal Justice System
       A.   The Police
       B.   The Courts
       C.   The Purposes of Punishment
       D.   Corrections
       E.   The Fundamental Dilemma of Criminal Justice

SUMMARY

➢   The legalistic approach defines crime as any violation of a law enacted by a
     legitimate government. In contrast, the natural law approach sees crime as a
     violation of some absolute principle.

➢   The United States follows the common law tradition in which numerous cases
     accumulate to form a coherent set of legal principles based on precedent. Many
     other societies embrace civil law or religious law traditions.

➢   Most sociologists rely on information from the Uniform Crime Reports (UCR) or
     from the National Crime Victimization Survey (NCVS), although both sources
     have serious weaknesses.

➢   Street crime has been declining in the United States since the early 1990s.
     Demographic changes and sharp increases in imprisonment help explain this
     trend.

➢   Rates of violent crime are much higher in the United States than in other
     developed countries, especially Japan.

➢   Homicides typically occur between people who know each other, often arising
     out of ongoing conflicts.

➢   Victims of rape receive more considerate treatment today than they did a few
     decades ago.

➢   Organized crime is often a means by which immigrants and minorities can
     succeed when legal opportunities are blocked.

➢   The four major types of corporate crime are financial offenses, maintaining
     hazardous working conditions, manufacturing unsafe products, and
     environmental crimes.

➢   Victimless crimes, created when the law attempts to prohibit the exchange
     between willing adults of strongly desired goods and services, are extremely
     difficult to control.

➢ Many nations, including the United States, are currently experimenting with community policing.

➢ American courts operate according to the adversarial principle, but in practice most cases are plea-bargained. In contrast, many European societies use the inquisitorial model.

➢ Punishment is based on one or more of four rationales: retribution, deterrence, rehabilitation, or incapacitation.

➢ The U.S. prison system has become enormously overcrowded over the past decade.

➢ Societies must choose an appropriate balance between short-run solutions to crime and long-run solutions that address crime's underlying causes.

➢ Persons who commit major street crimes tend to be young, lower-class males; a disproportionate number are members of minority groups. Most victims of street crimes come from the same demographic categories as do the offenders.

➢ The United States is virtually alone among the highly developed nations in using capital punishment.

➢ Some observers believe that the decriminalization of drug use would allow the criminal justice system to concentrate its energies and resources on more serious crimes.

MULTIPLE CHOICE

1. The definition of crime as "the violation of formal statutes established by legitimate governments" reflects which approach?

   a. rational
   b. legalistic
   c. natural law
   d. common law

2. Today, most advocates of the _____ approach see crimes as acts in opposition to supposedly universal principles of human rights.

   a. common law
   b. legalistic
   c. religious
   d. natural law

3. The legal system of the United States is grounded in the _____ -law tradition.

   a. civil
   b. religious
   c. common
   d. natural

4. Most of the world's societies follow the _____ -law tradition, which is *code* based.

   a. civil
   b. common
   c. religious
   d. natural

5. In Iran, criminal law is based on the Shari'a as revealed by Allah to the prophet Mohammed in the Qur'an and other writings. This reflects which "family" of criminal law?

   a. common
   b. religious
   c. civil
   d. natural

6. Eight street crimes, called _____ crimes, are given special attention in the Uniform Crime Reports.

   a. violent
   b. specialized
   c. heinous
   d. index

7. *Organized crime* is criminal activity conducted by

   a. average people.
   b. Sicilians.
   c. relatively large-scale and highly structured associations that routinely use corruption and violence to maximize their profits.
   d. all of the above

8. The general process whereby different national origin groups assume control of ethnic syndicates is termed

   a. ethnic succession.
   b. Sicilian takeover.
   c. la Cosa Nostra's revenge.
   d. international chaos.

9. Over fifty years ago, Edwin Sutherland directed sociologists' attention to a problem he called _____ crime.

   a. occupational
   b. corporate
   c. white-collar
   d. organized

10. *Embezzlement* committed by individuals against their employers is a type of _____ crime.

    a. organized
    b. occupational
    c. corporate
    d. misdemeanor

11. _____ crimes are criminal acts committed by businesses against their employees, customers, or the general public.

    a. Corporate
    b. Occupational
    c. Civil
    d. Misdemeanor

12.	_____ crimes are created when we use the criminal law to attempt to prohibit the exchange of strongly desired goods and services between willing adults.

    a. Common law
    b. Victimless
    c. Organized
    d. White-collar

13.	Common law societies, including the United States, structure their courts according to which principle?

    a. plea bargaining
    b. inquisition
    c. adversarial
    d. rehabilitation

14.	_____ is a system by which defendants plead guilty to a lesser charge rather than go to full trial.

    a. Inquisition
    b. Plaintiff's law
    c. Prosecutorial law
    d. Plea bargaining

15.	Unlike common law societies, civil law nations operate on which principle?

    a. adversarial
    b. inquisitorial
    c. plea bargaining
    d. retribution

16.	_____ deterrence is punishment of a particular individual intended to keep him or her from violating the law in the future.

    a. Rehabilitative
    b. General
    c. Specific
    d. Retributive

17.   _____ deterrence shows people who have yet to commit crimes what is done to offenders in the hope that they will decide not to break the law and be similarly punished.

   a. Rehabilitative
   b. Specific
   c. Retributive
   d. General

18.   It has been suggested that women, particularly white, working- and middle-class minor offenders, have historically been treated gently by the courts because of their gender. This view is known as the _____ hypothesis.

   a. double-standard
   b. chivalry
   c. pink-collar
   d. glass-ceiling

19.   Historically, criminologists focused almost exclusively on offenders, but during the last twenty years, a subfield of criminology has emerged, called

   a. rehabilitation.
   b. antiretribution.
   c. victimology.
   d. Environmentalism.

20.   Suppose that American society decided to legalize marijuana. This would be an example of

   a. decriminalization.
   b. retributive justice.
   c. plea bargaining.
   d. victimless alteration.

TRUE-FALSE

1.   No police-derived database will ever provide information about crimes that are not reported.

2.   All crime categories have declined dramatically since 1991.

3.   American violent crime rates are comparable to the rates in other postindustrial societies.

4. Approximately 50 percent of all index crimes fall into the category of violent crime.

5. Today, 90 percent of all rapes are never brought to the attention of the authorities.

6. Organized crime arose in the United States long before the immigration of large numbers of Italians.

7. The overall cost of corporate crime has been estimated to be *eighteen* times more costly (in terms of financial loss) in comparison with street crime.

8. In the past several decades, most American police departments have moved away from the model of *community policing*.

9. The bottom-line rationale that currently delineates correctional thinking in the United States is *rehabilitation*.

10. Crime is a random phenomenon.

ANSWERS - MULTIPLE CHOICE (correct answer/page reference)

1.	b	198
2.	d	198
3.	c	199
4.	a	199
5.	b	199
6.	d	200
7.	c	205
8.	a	205
9.	c	206
10.	b	206
11.	a	206
12.	b	207
13.	c	209
14.	d	209
15.	b	209-210
16.	c	210
17.	d	210
18.	b	215
19.	c	217
20.	a	221

<u>ANSWERS - TRUE-FALSE</u> (correct answer/page reference)

1.   T   200
2.   T   201
3.   F   201
4.   F   202
5.   F   203-204
6.   T   205
7.   T   207
8.   F   208
9.   F   211
10. F   213

CHAPTER 9
ECONOMIC STRATIFICATION

LEARNING OBJECTIVES

➢ To be able to identify where patterns of inequality based upon gender, age, race and ethnicity are the greatest.

➢ To see how systems of inequality are widely accepted by the members of society.

➢ To understand the role that ideology plays in economic inequality.

➢ To be able to identify how individual characteristics are seen to contribute to inequality.

➢ To be able to distinguish between the functional and conflict views of social inequality.

➢ To be able to identify the way multiple ranking systems contribute to change in the inequality.

➢ To understand the importance of status symbols in identifying the class of people.

➢ To learn the principal components of modernization, dependency, and world systems theory in the explanation of global stratification.

CHAPTER OUTLINE

I.   Legitimating Stratification
    A.   Ideology
    B.   Classism

II.   Systems of Economic Stratification

III.   Explaining Stratification
    A.   Deficiency Theory
    B.   Functional Theory
    C.   The Interactionist View

IV.   Global Stratification
      A.   Modernization Theory
      B.   Dependency Theory
      C.   World Systems Theory

SUMMARY

➢   All but the most traditional societies are characterized by patterns of social stratification based on variables such as gender, age, race or ethnicity, and economic status.

➢   Systems of social stratification are commonly legitimated by widely accepted belief systems termed ideologies.

➢   The ideology that legitimates economic inequality in modern societies may be called classism. It suggests that because there is widespread equal opportunity, both the wealthy and the poor deserve their fates.

➢   Structured economic inequality generally increases as societies develop until they reach the industrial stage, when this trend starts to reverse.

➢   Historic patterns of social stratification include slave and caste systems; contemporary developed societies emphasize class rather than more ascriptive patterns of structured economic inequality.

➢   Deficiency theories, generally regarded by sociologists as inaccurate and misleading, explain social stratification in terms of differences in individual ability.

➢   Functional theory, as developed in the Davis-Moore thesis, argues that economic stratification is inevitable and that it serves the positive function of ensuring that the most important statuses in society are filled by the most capable people.

➢   Conflict theorists disagree with the functional view that the effects of stratification are generally positive; some also deny that structured economic inequality is inevitable.

➢   Karl Marx believed social classes, composed of people who are a common relationship to the means of production, are locked in irreconcilable conflict with each other. In order to win this struggle, subordinate classes must attain class-consciousness; the dominant class attempts to retard class-consciousness by encouraging various forms of false consciousness.

➤   Ralf Dahrendorf had modified Marx's approach into a more general theory of struggle between dominant and subordinate groups in authority relationships.

➤   Max Weber identifies three overlapping systems of stratification in modern societies: economic classes, status groups, and parties or power groups.

➤   Symbolic interactionists emphasize the importance of status symbols and other ways that class differences influence everyday patterns of social interaction.

➤   The modern world displays a pattern of global stratification into several distinct groups of nations: fully developed, developing, and underdeveloped, or high-, medium- and low-income.

➤   Modernization theory suggests that all of the world's societies will eventually become fully developed.

➤   Dependency theory explains the poverty of many nations as a consequence of their economic domination by the developed world.

➤   World systems theory divides the world's nations into three categories—core, semiperiphery, and periphery—with each group playing a different role in a sort of global assembly line.

MULTIPLE CHOICE

1.   Sociologists use the term _____ in referring to the division of a large group or society into ranked categories of people, each of which enjoys different levels of access to scarce and valued resources, chiefly property, prestige, and power.

      a.   ethnic cleansing
      b.   social stratification
      c.   global categorization
      d.   international separation

2.   The _____ suggests that inequality mounts steadily as societies develop until they pass through the early phases of the industrial revolution, at which point it tends to decline.

      a.   functionalist theory of stratification
      b.   conflict theory of stratification
      c.   Kuznets curve
      d.   caste hypothesis

3.   _____ systems are made up of a number of sharply distinct groups whose membership is based entirely on ascription.

   a. Caste
   b. Class
   c. Functional
   d. Conflict

4.   Until recently, South Africa was characterized by a racial caste system called _____ that divided the population into distinct groups.

   a. ethnic cleansing
   b. racial purity
   c. genetic exclusion
   d. apartheid

5.   Industrial societies are characterized by _____ systems of stratification, based primarily on achievement rather than ascription and, hence, are relatively open, especially in the middle range.

   a. caste
   b. class
   c. closed
   d. apartheid

6.   _____ theories of stratification explain differences in property, power, and prestige as a direct consequence of individual differences in ability.

   a. Functionalist
   b. Conflict
   c. Interactionist
   d. Deficiency

7.   Herbert Spencer, who coined the phrase "survival of the fittest," fashioned a philosophy that was popular during the later nineteenth century, known as

   a. Social Darwinism.
   b. functionalism.
   c. symbolic interactionism.
   d. apartheid.

8. The _____ thesis maintains that inequality functions in motivating people to work hard and ensures that key statuses in society are occupied by highly capable people.

    a. Social Darwinist
    b. conflict
    c. Davis-Moore
    d. Parsons-Shils

9. Karl Marx described the economy as society's _____, the institution that shapes all the others.

    a. substructure
    b. superstructure
    c. proletariat
    d. bourgeoisie

10. For Karl Marx, government, family, education, philosophy, religion, art, literature, and virtually every other aspect of human life was part of the _____ of societies, because they are all influenced by the economy.

    a. substructure
    b. proletariat
    c. bourgeoisie
    d. superstructure

11. For Karl Marx, a society's _____ refers to whatever is used in that society to create wealth.

    a. substructure
    b. superstructure
    c. means of production
    d. class motivator

12. For Karl Marx, the capitalists, or "ruling class," are referred to as the

    a. proletariat.
    b. bourgeoisie.
    c. upper class.
    d. landed aristocracy.

13. For Karl Marx, the industrial workers, who have to sell their labor power on very disadvantageous terms in order to survive, are referred to as the

    a. serfs.
    b. lower class.
    c. bourgeoisie.
    d. proletariat.

14. According to Karl Marx, in order for a revolution to take place, the subordinate class must gain

    a. a substructural advantage.
    b. a superstructural advantage.
    c. class consciousness.
    d. control of the means of production.

15. Karl Marx stressed how religion strengthens _____ by encouraging poor people to focus on the supposed rewards of the next life instead of trying change things in the here-and-now.

    a. false class consciousness
    b. class consciousness
    c. the means of production
    d. the superstructure

16. For Weber, _____ was the ability of one social actor to compel a second social actor to behave in a way in which the latter would not otherwise have acted.

    a. authority
    b. political pull
    c. power
    d. cultural capital

17. _____ describes a situation in which an individual occupies several ranked statuses and some of them are evaluated more positively than others.

    a. Role conflict
    b. Status inconsistency
    c. Role strain
    d. Status anomie

18. _____ are external markers that allow people to identify and respond to the statuses occupied by others.

    a. Role identifiers
    b. Power components
    c. Labels
    d. Status symbols

19. In the decades following World War II, almost all colonial societies gained political independence, but they continued to be economically and technologically dependent upon the old colonial powers. Today, the colonial powers have been partially supplanted by vast multinational corporations. This pattern of continued dependency is known as

    a. neocolonialism.
    b. social dependency.
    c. colonialism.
    d. cultural imperialism.

20. The concept of _____ refers to people's opportunities to achieve positive goals such as good health, a nice home, and a rewarding family life.

    a. periphery
    b. core
    c. life chances
    d. semiperiphery

TRUE-FALSE

1. F   Social stratification does not exist on a global level.

2. T   In the context of social stratification, an *ideology* is a belief that legitimates existing patterns of structured social inequality.

3. F   Closed systems of stratification are heavily based on achieved statuses.

4. T   Open systems of stratification permit substantial upward and downward mobility.

5. T   The central point in Weber's analysis is that social stratification is *multidimensional*.

6. F   People are generally unaware of their membership in what Weber called status groups.

7. F Under colonialism, indigenous people were encouraged to govern themselves.

8. T Cultural imperialism refers to the continuing influence of high-income countries to keep the cultures of their former colonies from developing.

9. F In world systems theory, the *core* refers to former colonial nations whose primary role in the world economic system is to supply raw materials and labor for the global assembly line.

10. F In world systems theory, the *periphery* consists of high-income nations located mainly in Europe and North America.

ANSWERS - MULTIPLE CHOICE (correct answer/page reference)

1.	b	226
2.	c	229
3.	a	231
4.	d	233
5.	b	233
6.	d	234
7.	a	234
8.	c	235
9.	a	237
10.	d	237
11.	c	237
12.	b	237
13.	d	237
14.	c	237
15.	a	238
16.	c	241
17.	b	242
18.	d	242
19.	a	246
20.	c	248

ANSWERS - TRUE-FALSE (correct answer/page reference)

1.	F	226
2.	T	227
3.	F	229
4.	T	229
5.	T	239
6.	F	240
7.	F	246
8.	T	247
9.	F	248
10.	F	248

CHAPTER 1O
SOCIAL CLASS IN MODERN SOCIETIES

LEARNING OBJECTIVES

➤ To identify the major approaches used by sociologists to measure social class.

➤ To be able to distinguish among the dimensions of social class.

➤ To come to understand the change in wealth and income distribution in the United States.

➤ To begin to identify the differences among the social classes in the United States.

➤ To recognize the different types of social mobility in the United States and Europe and how these have affected the societies.

➤ To be able to distinguish the patterns of mobility that exist in modern societies.

➤ To be able to identify the way that social class shapes life chances and life styles.

➤ To recognize the myths and facts of poverty and welfare.

CHAPTER OUTLINE

I.   Measuring Class
      A.   The subjective approach
      B.   The reputational approach
      C.   The objective approach

II.   Property and Prestige: Two Dimensions of Class
      A.   Property
      B.   Occupational prestige

III. The American Class System
      A.   The upper class
      B.   The upper-middle class
      C.   The lower-middle class
      D.   The working class
      E.   The working poor
      F.   The "underclass"

IV.   Social Mobility

SUMMARY

➤ Most sociologists use the objective approach to operationalize the variable of class, although some prefer the subjective or reputational methods.

➤ Property—both income and wealth—is an important objective dimension of class. The gap between the rich and the poor, especially with regard to wealth, is greater in the United States than in other modern societies, and it is currently increasing.

➤ Occupational prestige is a second important objective factor separating social classes.

➤ Relational theorist Erik Olin Wright identifies four classes in U.S. society: capitalists, managers, the petit bourgeoisie, and workers.

➤ Disbributionalist theorists such as Gilbert and Kahl divide U.S. society into ranked groups: the upper, upper-middle, lower-middle, and working classes, the working poor, and the "underclass."

➤ Most social mobility in modern societies is structural rather than positional.

➤ The United States has historically offered substantial opportunities for upward social mobility, but recent trends suggest that downward mobility, especially out of the middle class, will be increasingly common in the immediate future.

➤ Social class strongly influences people's life chances regarding such matters as education, physical health and mortality, mental health, crime victimization, and self-esteem.

➤ Class also affects lifestyle patterns of child socialization, family life, politics, voluntary associations, religion, recreation and leisure, and communication styles.

➤ Poverty is usually defined in absolute terms, but some sociologists believe that a relative definition presents a more accurate image.

➤ The percentage of people living in poverty declined in the 1960s and early 1970s, but since then it has fluctuated at a somewhat higher level than previously.

➤ Poverty is concentrated among children, minorities, and women; it is an especially serious problem in single-parent, female-headed families.

➤ Sociologists find more support for system-blaming explanations of poverty than for kinds-of-people approaches such as the culture of poverty theory.

➤ Public policies concerning poverty can be categorized as anti-destitution, anti-poverty, or anti-welfare approaches.

➤ Research has found that many widely held beliefs about poverty are inaccurate. Nevertheless, these beliefs strongly influence public responses to the problem.

➤ The 1996 reform bill has substantially reduced welfare rolls, but it is unclear whether it will be effective in actually fighting poverty.

MULTIPLE CHOICE

1. The *subjective* approach to measuring class involves

   a. asking people to which class they think they belong.
   b. asking well-informed local "judges" to classify their fellow citizens into class categories.
   c. asking respondents for several facts about themselves and then using this information to place them in class categories.
   d. none of the above

2. Using the _____ approach, sociologists ask well-informed local "judges" to classify their fellow citizens into class categories.

   a. objective
   b. subjective
   c. reputational
   d. methodological

3. In the *objective* approach, sociologists ask

   a. people to which class they think they belong.
   b. well-informed local "judges" to classify their fellow citizens into class categories.
   c. ask respondents for several facts about themselves and then use this information to place them in class categories.
   d. none of the above

4. The most commonly used objective definition of class is called

    a. income flexibility.
    b. socioeconomic status.
    c. wealth.
    d. prestige.

5. Salaries, rents, interest, and dividends received from stocks and bonds are all examples of

    a. wealth.
    b. prestige.
    c. authority.
    d. income.

6. Net accumulated assets, including homes, land, automobiles, jewelry, factories, and stocks and bonds are all examples of

    a. wealth.
    b. income.
    c. prestige.
    d. authority.

7. In _____ terms, social classes differ solely with regard to their levels of income, wealth, education, occupational prestige, and power.

    a. functionalist
    b. relational
    c. distributionist
    d. interactionist

8. In _____ terms, social classes not only enjoy different levels of reward, but also occupy distinct structural positions within society's political economy.

    a. relational
    b. functionalist
    c. interactionist
    d. distributionist

9. A change in an individual or group's position in a stratification hierarchy is referred to as _____ mobility.

    a. structural
    b. social
    c. horizontal
    d. vertical

10. _____ social mobility refers to an individual's class position compared to that achieved by his or her parents or grandparents.

  a. Vertical
  b. Horizontal
  c. Structural
  (d.) Intergenerational

11. _____ social mobility refers to changes in an individual's social mobility social standing over his or her lifetime.

  a. Intergenerational
  (b.) Intragenerational
  c. Positional
  d. Structural

12. Jack's father is a bricklayer. Jack has become a corporate executive. This illustrates which type of mobility?

  a. intragenerational
  b. intergenerational
  c. vertical
  (d.) both b and c above

13. _____ mobility occurs when someone moves from one status to another that is roughly equal in rank.

  a. Positional
  b. Structural
  (c.) Horizontal
  d. Vertical

14. Most Americans think of mobility primarily as _____ mobility: They assume that people get ahead mainly because of their ability, dedication, and hard work.

  a. structural
  (b.) positional
  c. vertical
  d. horizontal

15. _____ mobility is generally a consequence of a change in the range of occupations that are available in a given society.

   a.) Structural
   b. Positional
   c. Intragenerational
   d. Intergenerational

16. _____ is a process in which the manufacturing sector of the economies of the developed nations declines while the service sector expands.

   a. Postindustrialization
   b. Structural improvement
   c.) Deindustrialization
   d. Globalization

17. The subcultural patterns that characterize the different classes are referred to as

   a.) life styles.
   b. permutations.
   c. life chances.
   d. occupations.

18. _____ poverty refers to a life-threatening lack of food, shelter, and clothing.

   a. Relative
   b.) Absolute
   c. Cultural
   d. Invisible

19. _____ poverty refers to situations in which individuals make substantially less than most of the people around them and who cannot afford purchases that most people take for granted are poor, even if they can afford the necessities of life.

   a.) Relative
   b. Absolute
   c. Cultural
   d. Invisible

20. The _____ refers to the increasing percentage of the poverty population that is made up of women.

   a. glass ceiling
   b. pink-collar ghetto
   c. velvet barrier
   (d.) feminization of poverty

TRUE-FALSE

1. T The top 5 percent of American families receive about 20 percent of all income in the United States.

2. T The United States has the most extreme income inequality in the developed world.

3. F The distribution of wealth in the United States is more equal than that of income.

4. T Members of the upper class generally feel a strong sense of class consciousness.

5. F Tracking in schools tends to be disassociated from class.

6. T The major social issue associated with class inequality is poverty.

7. T About two-thirds of all poor people are white, but minorities are disproportionately likely to be poor.

8. F The best single predictor of poverty is race/ethnicity.

9. F Sociologists have generally found that poor people are poor because they are lazy.

10. F The vast majority of government welfare spending is *means-tested*.

ANSWERS - MULTIPLE CHOICE (correct answer/page reference)

1. a 256
2. c 257-258
3. c 258
4. b 258
5. d 258
6. a 258
7. c 261
8. a 261
9. b 265
10. d 265
11. b 265
12. d 265
13. c 265
14. b 265
15. a 265
16. c 267
17. a 269
18. b 272
19. a 273
20. d 274

ANSWERS - TRUE-FALSE (correct answer/page reference)

1. T 258
2. T 258
3. F 259
4. T 262
5. F 269
6. T 272
7. T 273
8. F 274
9. F 275
10. F 276

CHAPTER 11
RACIAL AND ETHNIC MINORITIES

LEARNING OBJECTIVES

➤ To identify the roots of U.S. minority groups in immigration to the New World.

➤ To be able to state the factors that define a group as minority.

➤ To distinguish between the biological and social understandings of race.

➤ To learn the meaning of *prejudice* and *discrimination* and the differences between them.

➤ To discover racism in America.

➤ To be able to identify the different dominant-minority group relationships -- how dominant groups have dealt with minorities.

➤ To learn what the response of minorities has been to dominant groups.

➤ To discover the presence of involuntary minority groups around the world.

➤ To distinguish between voluntary and involuntary minority groups.

➤ To debate the intent of Affirmative Action.

CHAPTER OUTLINE

I.   From Immigrants to Migrants

II.   Defining Minority Groups
        A.   Race: A Social Concept
        B.   Ethnic Groups

III.   Prejudice, Discrimination, and Racism
        A.   Prejudice
        B.   Discrimination
        C.   Racism

IV.   Theories of Prejudice and Discrimination
        A.   Social Psychological Theories
        B.   Interactionist Theories
        C.   Functional Theories
        D.   Conflict Theories

V.   Patterns of Minority-Dominant Group Relations
        A.   Genocide
        B.   Expulsion and Population Transfer
        C.   Open Subjugation
        D.   Legal Protection -- Continued Discrimination
        E.   Assimilation
        F.   Pluralism
        G.   Minority Responses

SUMMARY

➢   Most Americans entered this country as immigrants. Since 1965, immigration from Latin America and Asia has been substantial. By the middle of the new century, only a numerical minority of Americans will be able to trace their ancestry back to Europe.

➢   Minority groups lack power compared to dominant groups. They also experience prejudice and discrimination, feel a sense of solidarity or peoplehood, are defined by ascription, and are usually endogamous.

➢   Although most people think of race as a biological concept, it is principally a social construct. Ethnic groups share a common subculture, somewhat distinct from the culture of the dominant group.

➢   Prejudice is a negative attitude toward an entire category of people. There are two components of prejudice: an emotional reaction and a cognitive stereotype.

➢   Discrimination consists of treating people differently on the basis of their category membership. It may be *de facto* or *de jure*; it may also be individual, direct institutional, or indirect institutional.

➢   Prejudice and discrimination often occur independently of each other.

- Racism is a widespread ideology that maintains one group is inherently superior to another.

- Prejudice and discrimination may result from personality-level processes, social learning, or economic conflict; they serve a number of functions as well as dysfunctions.

- Harmful patterns of dominant-minority group relations include genocide, expulsion, population transfer, open subjugation, and legal protection combined with *de facto* discrimination.

- Assimilation is a process whereby minorities shed their differences and adopt the characteristics of the dominant group. There are three levels of assimilation: cultural, structural, and biological.

- Under pluralism or multiculturalism, minorities retain their cultural identity yet peacefully coexist with other minorities and the dominant group.

- Some minority group members seek assimilation, some prefer pluralism, and others advocate separatism.

- African Americans and Native Americans in the Unites States and Catholics in Northern Ireland are examples of groups that became minorities involuntarily.

- Hispanics and Asian Americans in the United States and guest-workers in Germany are examples of groups that have become minorities principally through voluntary immigration.

- Affirmative action is a controversial policy designed to remedy the consequences of prior discrimination, generally through some sort of minority preferences.

MULTIPLE CHOICE

1. *Xenophobia* refers to an irrational fear of

    a. foreigners.
    b. heights.
    c. enclosed places.
    d. all minorities.

2. Above all else, a minority group is defined by its

    a. size.
    b. constituency.
    c. lack of power.
    d. appearance.

3. A/an _____ group is a category of people who are seen by themselves and others as sharing a distinct subculture, somewhat different from the culture of the dominant group.

    a. minority
    b. ethnic
    c. racial
    d. out

4. _____ is a negative attitude toward an entire category of people.

    a. Contempt
    b. Discrimination
    c. Ethnocentrism
    d. Prejudice

5. _____ refer(s) to broad overgeneralizations about a category of people that are applied globally, that is, to *all* members of the category.

    a. Stereotypes
    b. Stigmas
    c. Prejudices
    d. Discrimination

6.	_____ consists of treating individuals unequally and unjustly on the basis of their group memberships.

	a.	Prejudice
	b.	Symbolic racism
	c.	Discrimination
	d.	Ethnocentrism

7.	When discrimination is sanctioned or required by law, it is referred to as _____ discrimination.

	a.	de facto
	b.	direct institutional
	c.	individual
	d.	de jure

8.	_____ discrimination is based on custom.

	a.	De facto
	b.	De jure
	c.	Individual
	d.	Indirect institutional

9.	David refuses to hire a particular accountant because she is female and Hispanic. This best exemplifies which type of discrimination?

	a.	de jure
	b.	individual
	c.	de facto
	d.	direct institutional

10.	The officials at a particular university will not admit a disabled student because the university's buildings are not handicapped accessible. This best exemplifies which type of discrimination?

	a.	de jure
	b.	de facto
	c.	direct institutional
	d.	individual

11. _____ discrimination refers to policies that appear to be neutral or color blind, but in practice discriminate against minority groups.

   a. De jure
   b. De facto
   c. Individual
   d. Indirect institutional

12. The ideology maintaining that one race is inherently superior to another is referred to as

   a. discrimination.
   b. prejudice.
   c. racism.
   d. direct institutional discrimination.

13. _____ is the extermination of all or most of the members of a minority group.

   a. Annihilation
   b. Genocide
   c. Institutional elimination
   d. Involuntary suicide

14. When a dominant group views a minority as economically valuable, it is unlikely that the dominant group will kill or expel them. Instead, the dominant group commonly forces the minority into a situation called _____ wherein no pretense is made that the minority is in any way equal to the dominant group.

   a. open subjugation
   b. segregation
   c. assimilation
   d. amalgamation

15. The physical and social separation of dominant and minority groups is termed

   a. assimilation.
   b. amalgamation.
   c. segregation.
   d. open subjugation.

16. As dominant-minority relations improve, a real possibility arises of _____, the process by which minorities shed their differences and blend in with the dominant group.

    a. segregation
    b. amalgamation
    c. open subjugation
    d. assimilation

17. Intermarriage is referred to as biological assimilation or

    a. pluralism.
    b. amalgamation.
    c. open subjugation.
    d. institutional assimilation.

18. The final pattern of minority-dominant relations is _____, sometimes also called multiculturalism.

    a. pluralism
    b. amalgamation
    c. cultural assimilation
    d. structural assimilation

19. *Separatism* is a policy of voluntary structural and cultural isolation from the dominant group and is sometimes referred to as ethnic

    a. discrimination.
    b. prejudice.
    c. nationalism.
    d. assimilation.

20. Public and private efforts to recruit minorities and women into educational programs and jobs in which they have traditionally been under represented are referred to collectively as

    a. institutional rehiring.
    b. affirmative action.
    c. counterbalance discrimination.
    d. reverse discrimination.

TRUE-FALSE

1. The United States receives more immigrants each year than all the other countries in the world combined.

2. Most minority groups are based on *achieved* statuses and tend to be *exogamous*.

3. Both race and ethnicity are frequently master statuses.

4. The term *symbolic racism* is used to describe the behavior of dominant group members who do not appear overly prejudiced but who oppose programs that reduce racial inequality.

5. Scapegoats are people who deserve the blame for other people's problems.

6. According to the *contact hypothesis*, intergroup contact always heightens prejudice.

7. The *melting pot model* of assimilation suggests that various racial and ethnic groups came to this country and then lost their distinctiveness and "melted" into a single American category.

8. The *Anglo-conformity model* of assimilation suggests that immigrants maintain their ethnic identity, but live within a society of Anglos.

9. William Julius Wilson suggests that the key to understanding the plight of the ghetto poor lies in deindustrialization and the exodus of the black middle class.

10. Opponents of affirmative action argue that the practice is reverse discrimination.

ANSWERS - MULTIPLE CHOICE (correct answer/page reference)

1.	a	285
2.	c	287
3.	b	289
4.	d	289
5.	a	290
6.	c	291
7.	d	291
8.	a	291
9.	b	291
10.	c	291
11.	d	291
12.	c	292
13.	b	296
14.	a	297
15.	c	298
16.	d	298
17.	b	299
18.	a	299
19.	c	300
20.	b	309

ANSWERS - TRUE-FALSE (correct answer/page reference)

1.	T	284
2.	F	287
3.	T	289
4.	T	292
5.	F	293
6.	F	294
7.	T	298
8.	F	298
9.	T	302
10.	T	309

CHAPTER 12
GENDER ROLES

LEARNING OBJECTIVES

➢ To be able to expand on the social construction of gender.

➢ To identify the differences between conflict and functionalist perspectives on gender.

➢ To be able to identify the ways masculine and feminine are constructed.

➢ To see the importance of the family in shaping the gender of children.

➢ To understand how education reinforces and maintains the gender roles.

➢ To explain the distribution of men and women across occupations and the differences in reward for these occupations based upon gender.

➢ To explore the effects of development policy on gender around the world.

➢ To interpret the effect of media on gender.

➢ To consider the part played by government and religion in setting policy concerning gender inequality and the abortion rights debate.

CHAPTER OUTLINE

I.   Sex and Gender

II.   Theoretical Perspectives on Gender Roles
      A.   Functionalism
      B.   Conflict Theory
      C.   Symbolic Interaction
      D.   Feminist Sociological Theory: Linking Race, Class and Gender

III. Global Perspectives: Women in Development

IV.   Women's Economic Activities

V.   A Model of Women in Development

VI.   Gendered Social Institutions
        A.   Family Life
        B.   Education
        C.   Gender and the Workplace

VII.   Reducing Gender Stratification: Politics and the Law
        A.   Employment
        B.   Domestic Relations

SUMMARY

> In sociology, the term *gender* refers to the social, cultural, and psychological traits associated with males and females defining people as masculine or feminine. Because gender is learned, it varies between cultures, and changes over time as cultural definitions change.

> According to functionalist theory, pre-industrial societies adopted gender roles as a practical way of dividing up a family's labor. But in capitalist societies, conflict theorists claim, those traditional roles have become a source of gender inequality because women are not paid for domestic work.

> Symbolic interactionists view gender roles as social constructions based on how people define one another as masculine or feminine and then agree on those definitions.

> The family is an early and powerful source of gender socialization. Children as young as two years display gender roles learned through differences in the way parents interact with boys and girls.

> Throughout all levels of education, teachers respond differently to male and female students, reinforcing gender stereotypes.

> Mass media, from magazines to television and popular music, reinforce gender stereotypes and tend to portray women in domestic rather than professional roles and as sex objects. Men tend to be portrayed as powerful and aggressive.

> Women make a major economic contribution to society through their unpaid domestic work, which is undervalued. Outside the home, women who work for pay earn significantly less money than men because of gender-related attitudes.

> Despite federal legislation and affirmative action programs, the wage gap between men and women has narrowed only slightly over the past three-and-a-half decades, and gender discrimination in employment remains.

> Legal status regarding domestic relations between men and women tend to be based on traditional gender roles. Divorce law often favors husbands over wives in the disposition of property and the assignment of child support, and wives over husbands in the awarding of child custody.

> The abortion rights debate has become a battleground between religious conservatives, who uphold traditional gender roles, and feminists, who oppose gender inequality. The majority of the American public favors abortion rights.

MULTIPLE CHOICE

1. Sociologically, the biological characteristics distinguishing male and female are referred to as

   a. sex.
   b. gender.
   c. androgyny.
   d. hermaphrodite.

2. Sociologically, _____ refers to those social, cultural, and psychological traits linked to males and females through particular social contexts.

   a. sex
   b. gender
   c. androgyny
   d. androcentrism

3. The expected attitudes and behaviors a society associates with each sex are referred to as

   a. sex roles.
   b. androgyny.
   c. sex norms.
   d. gender roles.

4. _____ refers to the belief that one sex, female, is inferior to the other sex, male.

   a. Sexism
   b. Androcentrism
   c. Androgyny
   d. Functionalism

5.   Sexism is most prevalent in _____ societies where male-dominated social structures lead to the oppression of women.

       a.   apartheid
       b.   matriarchal
       c.   patriarchal
       d.   egalitarian

6.   Patriarchy goes hand in hand with _____, in which male-centered norms operate throughout all social institutions and become the standard to which all persons adhere.

       a.   sexism
       b.   elitism
       c.   functionalism
       d.   androcentrism

7.   Which theoretical perspective suggests that separate gender roles for women and men are beneficial?

       a.   functionalism
       b.   conflict
       c.   interactionism
       d.   developmentalism

8.   Which theoretical perspective reflects Marxian ideas about the relationship between the exploiter and the exploited?

       a.   functionalism
       b.   interactionism
       c.   conflict
       d.   developmentalism

9.   Which theoretical perspective asserts that gender is a social construction?

       a.   conflict
       b.   interactionism
       c.   functionalism
       d.   developmentalism

10. The inclusive world-wide movement to end sexism and sexist oppression by empowering women is termed

    a.   feminism.
    b.   egalitarianism.
    c.   comparable worth.
    d.   the velvet hammer.

11. Of the 1.3 billion people worldwide who live in poverty, _____ percent are women and girls.

    a.   40
    b.   50
    c.   60
    d.   70

12. In a model of women-in-development, which of the following is NOT essential?

    a.   It must be informed by sociological theory.
    b.   It is only useful if it translates meaningfully to practice.
    c.   It should avoid a feminist perspective.
    d.   It should be interdisciplinary.

13. Title _____ of the Educational Amendment Act of 1973 prohibits sex (gender) discrimination in schools receiving federal funds.

    a.   IX
    b.   X
    c.   XI
    d.   XII

14. The genders are not evenly distributed across occupations. When the majority of a particular occupation is made up of one gender, it becomes a normative expectation. This best illustrates

    a.   sexism.
    b.   gender-typing.
    c.   androgyny.
    d.   comparable worth.

15. According to the _____ model, if there is inequality in wages, it is due to individual choices in matters of education and occupation.

    a. human capital
    b. gender-typing
    c. wage gap
    d. retrofit

16. Regardless of how the wage gap is explained, its persistence is clearly linked to three factors. Which of the following is NOT one of these?

    a. The work women do is less valued overall.
    b. The higher the number of women in the occupation, the lower the wages; the converse is true for male-dominated occupations.
    c. Gender discrimination is largely in the minds of liberal feminists.
    d. Regardless of the law, gender discrimination in the workplace persists.

17. Women often fail to rise to senior-level positions because of invisible and artificial barriers constructed by male management. This condition has been described as the

    a. velvet hammer.
    b. pink-collar ghetto.
    c. feminists' lament.
    d. glass ceiling.

18. Title _____ of the 1964 Civil Rights Act makes it unlawful for an employer to refuse to hire, discharge, or discriminate against a person because of race, color, religion, sex, or national origin.

    a. VII
    b. VIII
    c. IX
    d. X

19. _____ is the idea that male and female jobs should be assessed according to skill level, effort, and responsibility.

    a. Egalitarianism
    b. Comparable worth
    c. Bonafide occupational qualification
    d. Apartheid

20. Legal statutes regarding wife-husband roles are based on three notions. Which of the following is NOT one of these?

   a. unity
   b. separate but equal
   c. shared partnership
   d. bonafide occupational qualification

TRUE-FALSE

1. Overall, the underlying cause of the inequality of women is that their roles are primarily domestic.

2. The first men's movement originated on college campuses in the 1970s as a reaction to the feminist movement.

3. For girls, elementary school is a negative influence.

4. Research demonstrates that elementary school teaches boys that problems are challenges to overcome; it often teaches girls that failure is beyond their control.

5. Male superiority in math is innate and this assertion has been documented repeatedly in research investigations.

6. Globally, the ratio of women to men in paid labor has declined about 25 percent since 1970.

7. Research consistently shows that even when controlling for education and work experience, and as measured by median annual earnings of full-time employees, women earn less than men.

8. Overall, research points out that men are paid more than women for what they do because men's work is consistently more valuable in comparison with women's work.

9. The acronym *BFOQ* stands for Basic Feminist Occupational Quotient.

10. In a *community property* state, all property acquired during a marriage is jointly owned by the spouses.

ANSWERS - MULTIPLE CHOICE (correct answer/page reference)

1. a   314
2. b   314
3. d   315
4. a   315
5. c   315
6. d   315
7. a   315
8. c   316
9. b   317
10. a   317
11. d   319
12. c   323
13. a   329
14. b   330
15. a   330-331
16. c   331
17. d   332
18. a   333
19. b   334
20. d   334

ANSWERS - TRUE-FALSE (correct answer/page reference)

1. T   319
2. T   324
3. F   327
4. T   327
5. F   328
6. F   329
7. T   330
8. F   331
9. F   334
10. T   334

CHAPTER 13
THE AGED AND SOCIETY

LEARNING OBJECTIVES

➤ To understand the various views of aging.

➤ To be able to discuss the impact of global graying.

➤ To identify the differences between the various sociological theories of aging.

➤ To learn the various aspects of aging in America.

➤ To list factors contributing to poverty in the aged.

➤ To understand the social problems associated with aging.

CHAPTER OUTLINE

I. The Process of Aging
   A. Defining Old Age
   B. Views from Other Disciplines
   C. Global Graying

II. Sociological Theories of Aging
   A. Disengagement Theory
   B. Activity Theory
   C. Continuity Theory
   D. Age Stratification Theory
   E. Symbolic Interaction theory

SUMMARY

➢ Old age is defined differently in various cultures. In Western cultures, old age is usually defined chronologically, but all cultures mark the aging process with role transitions.

➢ Aging is a natural process that is influenced by stresses such as emotions and health habits. *Primary aging* refers to the physical changes that accompany aging; *secondary aging* refers to the life stresses that involve how our bodies and minds react to the social effects of growing old, such as age prejudice.

➢ In general, old age is not associated with a significant decline in intelligence, nor with changes in personality. Psychological impairment is associated more with poor health and age prejudice.

➢ Alzheimer's disease is an organic brain syndrome characterized by progressively deteriorating mental functions. It is *not* a normal part of aging. Most people who suffer from Alzheimer's disease are in the oldest old category, age 85 and above.

➢ The elderly population is growing worldwide. Women outlive men all over the world. People are living longer and healthier, but care for the elderly toward the end of life strains resources of the developed world, which often relies on public funds for support.

➢ Disengagement theory sees successful aging as the voluntary, mutual withdrawal of the aged and society from each other. In contrast, activity theory sees successful aging as continuing the usual roles and substituting new ones if role loss occurs.

➢ Continuity theory, a social psychological perspective, suggests that adjustment to old age is an extension of earlier personality development. Race, gender, and SES affect the aging process more than personality.

➢ Age stratification theory emphasizes generational differences such as birth cohort in the aging process and the effects of separating the young and the old. Symbolic interaction theory emphasizes adaptation and choices of behavior in old age. It also focuses on ageism and the effects of labels on these choices.

➢ Most elderly people are married and express high life satisfaction. However, divorce and cohabitation are becoming more common. The remarriage rate is higher for elderly men; for both genders, remarriage is higher for the divorced compared to the widowed.

➢ Most Americans look forward to retirement. The most important determinants of satisfaction with retirement are health and financial status.

➢ The majority of elderly live in their own homes; only 5 percent are in long-term facilities. The loss of a spouse produces such emotional distress that the surviving spouse is more susceptible to illness and death, especially suicide among widowers.

➢ The poverty of the aged was cut in half by the advent of Medicare. Widows, racial minorities, and the oldest old are most likely to be poor.

➢ Women tend to be the primary caregivers for elderly parents and relatives. Because many are juggling responsibilities of parenthood and elder care, they have been dubbed the "sandwich generation."

➢ About 4 percent of the elderly are abused or neglected by spouses or caregivers in all settings. The elderly express a higher fear of crime but are less likely to be victims of crime than other age groups. However, they are at a higher risk for fraud.

➢ Many advocacy groups such as the Gray Panthers have been formed to combat ageism and promote positive thinking about the aged and the roles they can play in society.

MULTIPLE CHOICE

1. High school graduations and retirement dinners illustrate

   a. rites of passage.
   b. sacred rituals.
   c. religious ceremonies.
   d. social stigma.

2. The scientific study of aging is called

   a. scientology.
   b. zoology.
   c. exo-botany.
   d. gerontology.

3. _____ aging involves the physical changes that accompany our body's biological processes.

   a. Tertiary
   b. Secondary
   c. Primary
   d. Quaternary

4. _____ aging involves the lifetime of stresses our bodies are subjected to.

   a. Primary
   b. Secondary
   c. Tertiary
   d. Quaternary

5. *Alzheimer's disease* is a type of

   a. cancer.
   b. psychological problem.
   c. heart ailment.
   d. organic brain syndrome (OBS).

6. Countries with the highest proportion of the elderly are in which phase of the demographic transition?

   a. last
   b. middle
   c. first
   d. preliminary

7.	_____ theory views aging as the gradual, beneficial, and mutual withdrawal of the aged and society from one another.

	a.	Age stratification
	b.	Activity
	c.	Disengagement
	d.	Continuity

8.	Disengagement theory is an example of a classic _____ approach.

	a.	interactionist
	b.	developmental
	c.	conflict
	d.	functionalist

9.	_____ theory suggests that successful aging means not only that role performance and involvements continue, but that new ones are also developed.

	a.	Activity
	b.	Continuity
	c.	Disengagement
	d.	Age stratification

10.	_____ theory suggests that individual personality is important in adjusting to aging, with previously developed personality patterns guiding the individual's thinking and acting.

	a.	Activity
	b.	Continuity
	c.	Disengagement
	d.	Age stratification

11.	When a child is told to "act her age," this statement is made in relationship to what is expected for the _____ in her/his culture.

	a.	role structure
	b.	gender typing
	c.	age grade
	d.	age stratification

12. _____ theory seeks an understanding of how society makes distinctions based on age.

    a. Activity
    b. Disengagement
    c. Continuity
    d. Age stratification

13. When age and gender are combined so that the most powerful positions are assigned to the oldest men, a _____ exists.

    a. monopoly
    b. oligopoly
    c. gerontocracy
    d. autocracy

14. The devaluation and negative stereotyping of the elderly is termed

    a. ageism.
    b. a gerontocracy.
    c. age stratification.
    d. disengagement

15. The text points out that when elderly people are told that they are incompetent to do anything but "relax" in the rocking chair, they may never again be able to leave it. This illustrates how labeling can lead to

    a. a gerontocracy.
    b. social breakdown syndrome.
    c. disengagement.
    d. age stratification.

16. The theory of _____ takes into account the social categories that increase inequality throughout the life course.

    a. disengagement
    b. continuity
    c. age stratification
    d. cumulative disadvantage

17. The minority elderly face multiple jeopardy for poverty because

    a.   African Americans are forced from paid employment earlier in their careers earlier in their careers than whites, often because of poor health.
    b.   unemployment reduces pension and Social Security benefits.
    c.   their jobs often provide little in the way of economic security.
    d.   all of the above

18. Women are the primary caregivers to elderly parents, whether they are daughters or daughters-in-law. These women have been called the _____ generation because they are caught between caring for the older and younger generations at the same time.

    a.   odd-ball
    b.   beat
    c.   sandwich
    d.   bounce-around

19. It is estimated that _____ percent of all elderly people are abused each year in all settings.

    a.   4
    b.   8
    c.   12
    d.   21

20. Voluntary associations allow people to come together to work for morally worthwhile goals. On an international level, these associations are referred to a

    a.   advocacy groups.
    b.   nongovernmental organizations.
    c.   age stratification groups.
    d.   gospel organizations.

TRUE-FALSE

1.   Old age is positively associated with personality discontinuity.

2.   By the year 2025, *as a percentage of all elderly*, the United States will have the highest share of the oldest old in the world.

3. Most countries in the developing world have no real infrastructure that formerly supports services to their growing elderly population.

4. When profiling overall life of the elderly in the United States, the portrait that emerges is a negative one.

5. Of today's elderly, less than 5 percent have never married.

6. Research demonstrates consistently that the two critical factors in retirement satisfaction are health status and financial situation.

7. About 25 percent of the elderly are in continuous long-term care (nursing homes).

8. The role of *surrogate-parent* usually falls to the grandmother who cares for grandchildren while her daughter works.

9. As a group, the elderly have experienced a major increase in poverty since the 1960s.

10. Income increases with age among the elderly.

ANSWERS - MULTIPLE CHOICE (correct answer/page reference)

1.	a	345
2.	d	345
3.	c	345-346
4.	b	346
5.	d	348
6.	a	348
7.	c	351
8.	d	351
9.	a	353
10.	b	354
11.	c	355
12.	d	355
13.	c	355
14.	a	356

15.	b	357
16.	d	365-366
17.	d	366
18.	c	367
19.	a	368
20.	b	369

__ANSWERS - TRUE-FALSE__ (correct answer/page reference)

1.	F	347
2.	T	348
3.	T	350
4.	F	358
5.	T	358
6.	T	362
7.	F	364
8.	T	364
9.	F	366
10.	F	366

CHAPTER 14
THE FAMILY

LEARNING OBJECTIVES

➤ To be able to distinguish the functionalist, conflict, and feminist perspectives on the family.

➤ To contrast U.S. family structures with different global structures.

➤ To discuss the various aspects of love and marriage in the U.S.

➤ To understand the features of a successful marriage as well as some possible factors contributing to divorce.

➤ To discuss emerging lifestyles in the U.S.

➤ To be able to understand the differences in family life and structure among various ethnic groups.

➤ To be able to use the social perspective to discuss the causes and consequences of social change as it impacts the family.

CHAPTER OUTLINE

I.   Theoretical Perspectives on the Family: Function and Structure
    A.   Family Functions
    B.   Feminist and Conflict Critiques of Functionalism
    C.   Family Structure

II.   Global Perspectives
    A.   Marriage Forms and Residence Patterns
    B.   Communal Families

III. Love, Marriage, and Divorce—American Style
    A.   Mate Selection
    B.   Successful Marriages and Families
    C.   Divorce
    D.   Remarriage

IV.   Emerging Lifestyles
   A.   Singlehood
   B.   Cohabitation
   C.   Single-Parent Families
   D.   Egalitarian Marriages

SUMMARY

➤   The family is responsible for accomplishing important social functions including reproduction, regulation of sexual behavior, socialization, protection, and social placement. Functionalists argue that social stability is disrupted if families do not adequately carry out these functions.

➤   Feminists argue that viewing the patriarchal family as beneficial for social stability hampers the movement into egalitarian roles. Conflict theory focuses on how inheritance patterns keep wealth concentrated in the hands of a few families.

➤   Family structure has been altered by the processes of industrialization, urbanization, and overall modernization.

➤   Marriage patterns vary considerably across the globe. Multiple-spouse marriages, extended families, and communal families, such as the Israeli kibbutz, are examples.

➤   Rather than a purely emotional process, romantic love is structured. People fall in love with those who are similar to themselves (homogamy), especially in terms of race and age.

➤   Women tend to marry men who are higher in socioeconomic status. Women put a higher value on interpersonal understanding and men put a higher value on physical attractiveness in mate selection.

➤   Most couples express satisfaction in their marriages. Successful marriages and families have high levels of caring, communication, trust, loyalty, and emotional support.

➤   The United States has the highest divorce rate in the world. Although the divorce rate steadily increased throughout the twentieth century, it is leveling off.

➤   Teenage marriages among couples of lower socioeconomic status are the most likely to end in divorce. Marital permanence is helped when the couple is similar in age, race, religion, attitudes, and values.

➢ Divorce is a principle reason for the high poverty rate of single-parent women and their dependent children. No-fault divorce and joint custody contribute to the "feminization of poverty."

➢ The remarriage rate is lower for women than for men. Men are more likely to be free from sole custody and to have an age and economic advantage in remarrying.

➢ Many people are seeking alternatives to conventional household arrangements. Singlehood, cohabitation, and single-parent families are all increasing. Egalitarian marriages based on shared decision-making and nontraditional beliefs about gender are also increasing.

➢ America's multicultural heritage is reflected in its families. The four largest groupings are African American, Hispanic, Asian American, and Native American families. Their marriages and families are greatly influenced by their minority status.

➢ Intimacy and intensity of relationships lay the groundwork for family violence. Family violence is associated with low income, unemployment, alcohol use, drug abuse, and family isolation.

➢ Gay men and lesbians are challenging traditional views of marriage and family to receive benefits previously available only to married couples.

➢ The family values movement calls for a "family restorationist" model around the ideal of the patriarchal nuclear family. Sociological critiques of the model center on its failure to account for social change.

MULTIPLE CHOICE

1. In most societies, the family of _____ is established at marriage and is the culturally approved sexual union that legitimizes childbearing.

    a. orientation
    b. procreation
    c. generations
    d. indignation

2. The cultural norm in which people marry outside a particular group is termed

    a. heterogamy.
    b. endogamy.
    c. hypergamy.
    d. exogamy.

3. The family of _____ is the family in which children grow up and the vehicle for primary socialization.

   a. orientation
   b. procreation
   c. expression
   d. instrumentality

4. Traditional families usually assign the _____ role to the husband-father, who is expected to maintain the physical integrity of the family.

   a. expressive
   b. bilateral
   c. instrumental
   d. patrilineal

5. The wife-mother retains the _____ role and is expected to cement relationships and provide emotional support.

   a. instrumental
   b. expressive
   c. matrilineal
   d. matriarchal

6. _____ is a cultural norm in which people marry within certain groups, with social class, race, and religion among the most important elements.

   a. Exogamy
   b. Heterogamy
   c. Endogamy
   d. Homogamy

7. Which form of descent uses both parents to trace family lines and is most common in Western societies?

   a. bilateral or bilineal
   b. patrilineal
   c. matrilineal
   d. egalitarian

8. Typical in rural areas globally are _____ families, consisting of parents, dependent children, and other relatives, usually of at least three generations, living in the same household.

   a. nuclear
   b. modified extended
   c. chosen
   d. extended

9. _____ families consist of wife, husband, and their dependent children who live apart from other relatives in their own residence.

   a. Nuclear
   b. Modified extended
   c. Extended
   d. Chosen

10. Most Western societies enforce _____, marriage to one spouse at a time.

    a. polygamy
    b. polygyny
    c. monogamy
    d. polyandry

11. _____ means marriage to more than one spouse at a time.

    a. Monogamy
    b. Polygyny
    c. Polyandry
    d. Polygamy

12. Suppose that a newly married couple moves into the husband's home. This reflects which pattern of residence?

    a. matrilocal
    b. patrilocal
    c. neolocal
    d. bilocal

13. Suppose that a newly married couple moves into the wife's home. This reflects which pattern of residence?

    a. bilocal
    b. neolocal
    c. patrilocal
    d. matrilocal

14. The most common form of plural marriage is

    a. polygyny.
    b. polygamy.
    c. polyandry.
    d. hypergamy.

15. A rare form of plural marriage found in about 1 percent of the world's societies involves a woman marrying more than one man at a time. This pattern is termed

    a. polygyny.
    b. polygamy.
    c. polyandry.
    d. hypergamy.

16. Becoming attracted to and marrying someone similar to yourself is termed

    a. homogamy.
    b. hypergamy.
    c. heterogamy.
    d. monogamy.

17. _____ refers to the process in which women tend to marry men of higher socioeconomic status.

    a. Homogamy
    b. Hypergamy
    c. Exogamy
    d. Endogamy

18. The marriage-divorce-remarriage pattern is called

    a. blended family.
    b. reconstituted family.
    c. serial monogamy.
    d. remarriage.

19. Remarriages are the primary reasons for the formation of _____ families, in which children from parents' prior relationships are brought together in a new family.

    a. extended
    b. nuclear
    c. modified extended
    d. blended

20. In a/an _____ marriage, partners share decision making and assign family roles based on talent and choice rather than on traditional beliefs about gender.

    a. egalitarian
    b. patriarchal
    c. matriarchal
    d. bilateral

TRUE-FALSE

1. The family is a cultural universal and the oldest, most conservative of the social institutions.

2. In societies that use bilateral or bilineal descent, inheritance by sons and male kin is guaranteed.

3. The most common pattern of tracing inheritance is matrilineal descent.

4. A modified-extended family consists of a father, a mother, and dependent children, who all live in the same household.

5. Communes are collective households where people who may or may not be related share roles typically associated with families.

6. The *kibbutz* is a form of Japanese family in which married couples share a residence.

7. A *marriage squeeze* refers to a time period in a society when marriage is unpopular.

8. Contrary to media stereotypes, sociological research consistently documents that marriage is what most people want and that they are happy with their choices.

9. The vast majority of both genders marry, but the percent of never-married people continues to increase, especially for women.

10. Since 1970, the number of single-parent households has doubled, a figure that includes the 60 percent of divorced couples with children.

ANSWERS - MULTIPLE CHOICE (correct answer/page reference)

1.	b	374
2.	d	374
3.	a	375
4.	c	375
5.	b	375
6.	c	375
7.	a	375
8.	d	377
9.	a	377
10.	c	378
11.	d	378
12.	b	378
13.	d	378
14.	a	378
15.	c	379
16.	a	380
17.	b	382
18.	c	386
19.	d	386
20.	a	389

ANSWERS - TRUE-FALSE (correct answer/page reference)

1. T 374
2. F 375
3. F 375
4. F 378
5. T 378
6. F 379
7. F 381
8. T 383
9. T 387
10. T 388

CHAPTER 15
EDUCATION

LEARNING OBJECTIVES

➢ To list the functions of education according to the functionalist perspective.

➢ To understand the inequalities in education according to the conflict perspectives.

➢ To discuss the symbolic interactionist perspective of education.

➢ To discuss ways to enhance student achievement.

➢ To compare and contrast global views of education.

➢ To be able to distinguish the conflicting views regarding the necessity of multicultural education.

➢ To understand the impact of multiculturalism and global interdependence on education.

➢ To understand the social issues surrounding diversity in education.

CHAPTER OUTLINE

I.   Sociological Perspectives on Education
     A.   Functionalism and the Functions of Education
     B.   Conflict Theory and Educational Inequality
     C.   Symbolic Interaction: Education as Socially Constructed
     D.   Applying Sociological Theory to Education

II. A Global View of Education

SUMMARY

➤ In the United States, education helps to unify a diverse society. It socializes children, helps the children of foreign-born parents to assimilate into mainstream society, and prepares the younger generation to adapt to a rapidly changing culture and economy.

➤ While functionalists see the schools as nurturers of talent and ability, regardless of a child's social class, conflict theorists charge that the schools reinforce the social-class structure. Social class is, in fact, the best overall indicator of educational achievement.

➤ American schools mirror the communities in which they are located: some are well staffed, well furnished, and well maintained while others are run-down, ill equipped, and poorly staffed. Thus, students from poor communities are at a disadvantage.

➤ Research shows that within American schools, students are distributed to different academic levels based more on their class, race, and gender than on their ability or past achievement.

➤ According to symbolic interaction theory, assigning students to lower levels, or tracks, reduces their self-esteem and their motivation to achieve. To avoid these effects, educators have adopted a policy of mainstreaming, including special-needs students in classrooms whenever possible.

➤ A society's educational level affects its level of economic development, its marriage and birthrates, and its income and nutritional levels. Because education has such a profound effect on people's living conditions, it is a powerful agent of social change.

➤ Demographers predict that by the year 2025, slightly more than half the students in U.S. classrooms will be people of color. The realization that the racial and ethnic makeup of the nation's schools is changing has produced a paradigm shift in educational policy, away from a Western, or Eurocentric, model and toward a multicultural curriculum.

➤ Though the student bodies at four-year colleges and universities have become more diverse in terms of their age, race, religion, ethnicity, and nationality, most are still drawn disproportionately from the middle and upper classes. Women, racial minorities, and working and lower-class students are overrepresented at community colleges.

➤ Busing of students was instituted to remedy inequalities in the school related to racial segregation. But it has not eliminated school segregation, and its educational results have been mixed.

➤ Over the last three decades, standardized test scores declined and functional illiteracy increased among American students. Educational reformers are seeking to improve these results through a "back to basics" approach and standards-based competency testing.

MULTIPLE CHOICE

1. Which of the following is NOT one of the four functions of education mentioned in the text?

   a. education as socialization
   b. education as transmission of culture
   c. education as innovation
   d. education as a tracking device

2. The role of education as a transmitter of culture also involves the function of _____, where children from many diverse cultures and subcultures are transformed to committed Americans.

   a. amalgamation
   b. tracking
   c. assimilation
   d. reification

3. Society rewards people on the basis of ability and achievement—on what they can do—and the school is a microcosm of society. This illustrates the idea of

   a. amalgamation.
   b. meritocracy.
   c. credentialism.
   d. tracking.

4. _____ involves an individual's qualification for a job or social status being based on the completion of some aspect of formal education.

   a. Credentialism
   b. Meritocracy
   c. Amalgamation
   d. Tracking

5.	_____ functions are those consequences of social life that are explicit, intended, and recognized.

   a.	Latent
   b.	Dys-
   c.	Manifest
   d.	Meta-

6.	_____ functions are unintended and may remain unrecognized.

   a.	Manifest
   b.	Dys-
   c.	Meta-
   d.	Latent

7.	Which of the following is NOT a recognized *dysfunction* of education?

   a.	Education transmits culture, but what is transmitted and how it is transmitted has created tension among various groups.
   b.	Schools provide social networks.
   c.	Bringing masses of youngsters together as peers has contributed to a weakening of parental authority.
   d.	Inflexible school bureaucracy and teacher demands may interfere too much in a family's life.

8.	_____ theory focuses on the social placement function of education and argues that a principal function of schooling in the United States is to reproduce and reinforce inequality.

   a.	Conflict
   b.	Functionalist
   c.	Interactionist
   d.	Developmental

9.	The _____ includes all the informal, unwritten norms that schools use to keep students in line.

   a.	hidden curriculum
   b.	school revolution
   c.	backstage agenda
   d.	invisible ceiling

10. The practice of grouping children according to an assessment of their ability is called

    a. credentialism.
    b. meritocracy.
    c. tracking.
    d. amalgamation.

11. The modification of behavior by the student illustrates the symbolic interactionist concept of _____ –new labels produce new behavior in an ongoing process.

    a. mainstreaming
    b. tracking
    c. the hidden curriculum
    d. the end point fallacy

12. _____ refers to the integration of special-needs students into the overall classroom or school, and recognizes the power of labeling.

    a. The end point fallacy
    b. Mainstreaming
    c. Tracking
    d. The hidden curriculum

13. According to the text,

    a. families provide different levels of encouragement for their children to succeed in school.
    b. school funding rises and falls according to interests by politicians and the health of the economy.
    c. the whole social system and not just small pieces of it must be part of the process to improve student learning.
    d. all of the above

14. The text points out that multicultural studies have impacted every level of education. This impact is so profound that it is associated with a rather rare and exciting event in scholarship, that of a/an _____, in which a dominant theory becomes directly competitive with, or is replaced by, another theory.

    a. paradigm shift
    b. retrospective
    c. end point fallacy
    d. hidden curriculum

15. Which U.S. Supreme Court Court case established the doctrine of "separate but equal," which protected racial segregation in public schools?

    a.   *Brown v. Board of Education of Topeka*
    b.   *Roe v. Wade*
    c.   *Plessy v. Ferguson*
    d.   *Miranda v. Arizona*

16. Which watershed U.S. Supreme Court case said that segregated schools are "inherently" unequal?

    a.   *Brown v. Board of Education of Topeka*
    b.   *Roe v. Wade*
    c.   *Plessy v. Ferguson*
    d.   *Miranda v. Arizona*

17. Current busing activities have been expanded to include busing inner-city, African-American children to mostly white suburban districts and busing white children to newly created inner-city _____ schools.

    a.   tarmac
    b.   magnet
    c.   random
    d.   white flight

18. The inability to do the reading, writing, or basic math necessary to carry out daily activities is termed

    a.   retardation.
    b.   learning disability.
    c.   Downs' syndrome.
    d.   functional illiteracy.

19. Both the Bush and Clinton administrations have advocated which of the following goals?

    a.   The United States should have a 90 percent high school graduation rate.
    b.   A certain amount of illiteracy must be tolerated.
    c.   Competence testing in core subjects should be abandoned.
    d.   It is not critical that the United States be first in math and science achievement.

20. According to the text, which of the following is NOT one of the sound sociological components of a model for educational reform?

    a.   empowered parents
    b.   a responsive workplace
    c.   the elimination of television as a teaching tool
    d.   neighborhoods for learning

TRUE-FALSE

1.   Modern functionalism says of education that while the schools have problems, the educational system as a whole is doing its job.

2.   Schooling is supposed to enhance opportunities for all to succeed but conflict theory suggests that it actually does the opposite.

3.   Conflict theorists argue that tracking encourages equal opportunity.

4.   The text points out that a self-fulfilling prophecy is a completely passive process.

5.   Of all social institutions, education perhaps best illustrates the application of sociological theory to the real world.

6.   The text observes that one of the best ways to ensure a country's overall well-being is to teach girls to read.

7.   Businesses are reluctant to hire graduates who come from programs that are *too* skill-based.

8.   White flight to the suburbs has been totally unrelated to busing.

9.   In almost all measures, achievement levels of American children are far lower than those in many other nations.

10.   At the individual level, there is no difference between a child's readiness to learn and her or his opportunity to learn.

ANSWERS - MULTIPLE CHOICE (correct answer/page reference)

1.	d	403-406
2.	c	404
3.	b	405
4.	a	405
5.	c	406
6.	d	406
7.	b	406
8.	a	407
9.	a	407
10.	c	408
11.	d	410
12.	b	410
13.	d	412
14.	a	417
15.	c	422
16.	a	422
17.	b	423
18.	d	425
19.	a	427
20.	c	428

ANSWERS - TRUE-FALSE (correct answer/page reference)

1.	T	407
2.	T	408
3.	F	409
4.	F	410
5.	T	412
6.	T	413
7.	T	421
8.	F	424
9.	T	425
10.	F	428

CHAPTER 16
RELIGION

LEARNING OBJECTIVES

➤   To be able to compare and contrast the functionalist, conflict, and rational choice theories regarding their views of religion.

➤   To understand the differences between various expressions of religious belief.

➤   To distinguish between the major types of religious organizations: church, denomination, sect, and cult.

➤   To gain an understanding of the major world religions.

➤   To discuss the roots and impact of global fundamentalism as well as Christian fundamentalism.

➤   To be able to trace the development from goddess-centered to more patriarchal religions.

➤   To understand the coexistance of religiosity and secularization in America.

➤   To understand the differences between Protestants, Catholics, and Jews in America.

CHAPTER OUTLINE

I.   Theoretical Perspectives on Religion
     A.   Functionalism
     B.   Functions of Religion
     C.   Conflict Theory and Social Change
     D.   Rational Choice Theory

II. Religious Beliefs and Organization
     A.   Expressions of Religious Belief
     B.   Types of Religious Organization

III.   World Religions and Social Change
        A.   Christianity
        B.   Islam
        C.   Judaism
        D.   Hinduism
        E.   Ethicalist Religions—Buddhism and Confucianism

IV.   Global Fundamentalism

SUMMARY

➤   According to Emile Durkheim, religion performs several social functions. A source of social cohesion and social control, religion promotes social service, offers believers strength and community in time of crisis, gives meaning to life by addressing the ultimate questions of life and death.

➤   Max Weber challenged this and argues that religion served as an incentive for the rise of capitalism and promoted social change.

➤   Anthropologists originally argued that religion evolved through stages, from lower- to higher-level forms: animism (supernatural beings and spirits that can help or hurt) to theism, belief in many gods, (polytheism) to one god (monotheism). This evolutionary view is no longer accepted by social scientists.

➤   A church is an inclusive structure with a specific theology and professionally-trained clergy. Some societies have ecclesia, or state religion. Churches may be split into denominations, separate branches that emphasize different interpretations of the same theology. Denominations are typical in societies with high religious pluralism.

➤   While churches are integrated into the larger society, sects are small, relatively informal groups, many of whose members have experienced a religious conversion. Sects often split away from established churches.

➤   Cults are small groups of believers who begin new or unconventional religions, usually founded by a charismatic leader. Most cults have little formal organization; they seldom survive beyond their leaders' lifetimes.

➤   Christianity, Judaism, and Islam share common roots. Both Christianity and Islam began as monotheistic cults centered around charismatic leaders; both survived to become world religions.

➤ Hinduism is the oldest of the world religions, and is polytheistic, with a belief in reincarnation. India's caste system is consistent with many Hindu beliefs, such as reincarnation and dharma (service to others).

➤ Buddhism and Confucianism, which originated in Asia, are based on ethical codes intended to promote human happiness and a higher state of consciousness. Both religions emphasize self-discipline.

➤ Fundamentalism is a religious trend found in all world religions; it seeks to curb social change and modernization and return society to a previous golden age. Some fundamentalists are political activists and desire a religious state. Others desire to be left alone to practice their religion with no interference.

➤ The most ancient religions were goddess-centered, and many of the world's great religions once treated women more as the equal than the inferior of men. Over time, however, men used patriarchal institutions to exclude women from religious leadership and reduce their social status.

➤ Founded on the principles of religious tolerance and the separation of church and state, the United States is the most religiously pluralistic society in the world. Most Americans are affiliated with religions and believe in God. However, strong secularization also exists, such as faith in science rather than religion for problem solving.

➤ American Protestants are divided into many denominations. Mainstream Protestants tend to be upwardly mobile and politically liberal, while fundamentalist Protestants tend to be poor and more politically conservative.

➤ Like mainstream Protestants, Roman Catholics have declined in religious commitment and are more diverse than in the past. They include both liberals who approve of birth control and the ordination of women and traditionalists who profess rigorous adherence to papal proclamations.

➤ Only about 2 percent of Americans are Jewish; most live in metropolitan areas. As a group, Jews are well educated and earn high incomes; politically liberal, they are politically influential.

➤ The New Christian Right is a coalition of fundamentalist groups that seeks to incorporate Christian principles into government policy. It generally opposes abortion rights, sex education in public schools, and the Equal Rights Amendment. It favors prayer and teaching creationism in public schools.

MULTIPLE CHOICE

1. _____ is the process in which religion, challenged by science and modernization, loses its influence on society, thereby threatening its own existence.

   a. Religious pluralism
   b. Theological departure
   c. Secularization
   d. Spiritual separation

2. _____ refers to a movement designed to revitalize faith by returning to the traditional ways the religion was practiced in the past.

   a. Religious pluralism
   b. Fundamentalism
   c. Secularization
   d. Theological revitalization

3. When many religions are tolerated in a society and these groups are often in competition with one another for members, this condition is referred to as

   a. religious pluralism.
   b. functional conflict.
   c. fundamental conflict.
   d. theological strife.

4. Sociologist Émile Durkheim defined *religion* as

   a. the opiate of the masses.
   b. a departure from the profane.
   c. theological reason.
   d. a unified system of beliefs and practices relative to sacred things.

5. *Theology* is best defined as

   a. a form of supernaturalism.
   b. a form of fundamentalism.
   c. a systematic formulation of religious doctrine.
   d. a collection of sacred rituals.

6. According to Durkheim, the realm of the _____ are set apart from the everyday world, inspire awe and reverence, and are often imbued with transcendent qualities.

   a. profane
   b. sacred
   c. supernatural
   d. magical

7. According to Durkheim, the realm of the _____ consists of everyday objects.

   a. mundane
   b. banal
   c. profane
   d. insane

8. Which of the following is NOT one of the functions of religion discussed in the text?

   a. Religion is a significant source of social cohesion.
   b. People find strength, comfort, and support through religion.
   c. Religion bolsters emotional well-being by addressing "ultimate" questions.
   d. All of the above are functions of religion.

9. _____ involves the belief that supernatural beings or spirits capable of helping or hurting people inhabit living things and inanimate objects.

   a. Animism
   b. Theism
   c. Polytheism
   d. Monotheism

10. The belief in one or more independent supernatural beings (gods) who do not exist on earth and who are more powerful than people is termed

    a. animism.
    b. polytheism.
    c. the civil religion.
    d. theism.

11. The belief in many gods is referred to as

    a. theism.
    b. the civil religion.
    c. polytheism.
    d. animism.

12. The belief in one all-powerful, all-knowing god is termed

    a. theism.
    b. monotheism.
    c. animism.
    d. the civil religion.

13. The concept of _____ describes a system of values associated with sacred symbols that is integrated into the broader society and shared by the society's members, regardless of their individual religious affiliations.

    a. civil religion
    b. animism
    c. monotheism
    d. church

14. Another term for *secular religion* is

    a. animism.
    b. monotheism.
    c. civil religion.
    d. ecclesia.

15. _____ is an inclusive religious body that brings together a moral community of believers in formalized worship and accommodates itself to the larger secular world.

    a. An ecclesia
    b. A denomination
    c. A sect
    d. A church

16. When a church is institutionalized as a formal part of a state or nation and claims citizens as members, it is a/an

    a. denomination.
    b. ecclesia.
    c. sect.
    d. cult.

17. Used in the context of religious pluralism, a/an _____ is a socially accepted and legally recognized body with bureaucratic characteristics similar to a church.

    a. ecclesia
    b. sect
    c. denomination
    d. cult

18. _____ are smaller religious groups and either aloof or hostile to the secular society surrounding them.

    a. Sects
    b. Cults
    c. Denominations
    d. Ecclesias

19. _____ usually organize around a charismatic leader who provides the basis for a new, unconventional religion, with no clearly defined structure and a great deal of tension with the larger society.

    a. Sects
    b. Cults
    c. Ecclesias
    d. Denominations

20. _____ is a fundamentalist political movement composed of a number of mostly Protestant conservative pressure groups with an agenda calling for returning morality to American society.

    a. Jehovah's Witnesses
    b. The Church of the Latter-Day Saints
    c. The Moon Unification Church
    d. The New Christian Right

TRUE-FALSE

1. Rational choice theory applies a marketplace approach to religion, assuming that people's choice of religion will be determined by its costs and benefits to them.

2. Regardless of focus, the attraction of new members to cults rests with the charisma of the leader.

3. The world's second largest and fastest growing religion is Buddhism.

4. Christianity, Islam, and Hinduism all involve efforts to proselytize: to gain adherents through concerted efforts to convert others to the religion.

5. All world religions exhibit some fundamentalist trends.

6. The United States has the lowest degree of religious pluralism in the world.

7. The United States is second only to Ireland and Italy in levels of religious affiliation and religious belief.

8. Schisms discourage religious pluralism.

9. By definition, the American Jewish congregation is an ethnic congregation.

10. The rise of Christian fundamentalism suggests a lack of support for the secularization hypothesis and demonstrates that religious pluralism is alive and well in American society.

ANSWERS - MULTIPLE CHOICE (correct answer/page reference)

1.	c	432
2.	b	432
3.	a	432
4.	d	432
5.	c	432
6.	b	432
7.	c	432
8.	d	433
9.	a	436
10.	d	436
11.	c	436
12.	b	436
13.	a	437

14.	c	437
15.	d	437
16.	b	438
17.	c	438
18.	a	438
19.	b	438
20.	d	455

ANSWERS - TRUE-FALSE (correct answer/page reference)

1.	T	436
2.	T	438
3.	F	442
4.	F	443
5.	T	446
6.	F	448
7.	T	448
8.	F	450
9.	T	454
10.	T	457

CHAPTER 17
THE POLITICAL ECONOMY

LEARNING OBJECTIVES

➤ To be able to distinguish the three types of power and the three types of authority.

➤ To understand the major normative perspectives on political economy: liberalism, socialism, and conservatism.

➤ To understand the four models of political economy and how they are linked with the three major sociological perspectives.

➤ To discuss the types of economic systems and how they are related to various political structures.

➤ To understand the possible reasons for voter apathy in the U.S.

➤ To discuss the issues surrounding nuclear proliferation.

CHAPTER OUTLINE

I.   Power and Authority
     A.   Three Types of Power
     B.   Three Types of Authority
     C.   Maintaining the Stability of Authority

II. Theories of the Political Economy
     A.   Normative Perspectives on the Political Economy
     B.   Empirical Perspectives on the Distribution of Political Power

III. Contemporary Political Economies
     A.   Economic Systems
     B.   Political Systems
     C.   Political Economies in the Real World

SUMMARY

- The concept of a political economy emphasizes the fact that the economic and political institutions of modern societies are largely inseparable from one another, especially at the higher levels.

- Power is the ability to compel others to act as the powerholder wishes, even if they attempt to resist. There are three types of power: decision-making power, agenda control, and systemic power.

- Authority is legitimate power. Max Weber identified three ideal types of authority: traditional, rational-legal, and charismatic.

- Claimants normally attempt to maintain their authority be means of a legitimating ideology. They also rely on the support of other institutional elites.

- There are three major images of the ideal form of political economy: liberalism, socialism, and conservatism.

- There are four competing models of the actual distribution of political power in modern societies: pluralism, the power-elite model, the ruling-class model, and state-autonomy theory.

- Some modern economic systems are primarily capitalist, some are socialist, and some, termed mixed economies or social democracies, are intermediate between the two polar types.

- Political regimes may be authoritarian or democratic. Types of authoritarian regimes include monarchies, patrimonial regimes (dictatorships), bureaucratic-authoritarian regimes, and totalitarian states. Democratic regimes may be either participatory or representative democracies.

- In most cases, the transition from authoritarianism to democracy is instigated by elites, although sometimes it is promoted by the lower classes.

- Citizens in democratic societies sometimes resort to nonviolent political protest to make their views known. Some oppositional groups and governments engage in terrorism, the use or threat of violence as a political strategy.

- Voter turnout in the United States is exceptionally low. In part, this may be explained by structure of the American political institution, especially the two-party system. It also reflects the low levels of confidence Americans express for most major social institutions.

➢ As the world has globalized, local and state governments have begun to compete against each other to attract international businesses.

➢ Nuclear proliferation is one of the most serious problems currently facing the world's societies.

MULTIPLE CHOICE

1. Traditionally, *politics* involves the struggle for control of the _____, the institution that maintains a monopoly over the legitimate use of force within a given territorial area.

    a. political economy
    b. state
    c. corporation
    d. multinational

2. In studying the political economy, the most important concept is

    a. money.
    b. prestige.
    c. power.
    d. status.

3. Power that is widely perceived by subordinates as fair and just is termed

    a. reasonable domain.
    b. imminent domain.
    c. leverage.
    d. authority.

4. _____ authority is power legitimated by respect for long-established cultural patterns.

    a. Traditional
    b. Rational-legal
    c. Charismatic
    d. Routinized

5. Power legitimated by legally enacted rules and regulations reflects which type of authority?

   a. routine
   b. charismatic
   c. traditional
   d. rational-legal

6. _____ authority is based on a claim to possess extraordinary or unique leadership abilities.

   a. Traditional
   b. Rational-legal
   c. Charismatic
   d. Routinized

7. A situation in which a single provider dominates the market and reaps windfall profits is referred to as a/an

   a. oligopoly.
   b. monopoly.
   c. oligarchy.
   d. hierarchy.

8. The central idea of _____ is that collective control of the economy reduces inequality and social injustice and contributes to peace and prosperity.

   a. socialism
   b. communism
   c. capitalism
   d. conservatism

9. _____ mandates the communal or collective ownership of all property.

   a. State socialism
   b. Communism
   c. Socialism
   d. Democracy

10. Most modern liberals espouse _____, the view that competition among elites disperses power among a number of different individuals and groups.

    a. capitalism
    b. socialism
    c. autonomy
    d. pluralism

11. _____ maintains that real power is concentrated in the hands of a small and relatively cohesive group of bureaucratic elites.

    a. Pluralism
    b. The ruling class thesis
    c. Elite theory
    d. The state autonomy thesis

12. The practice of simultaneously holding seats on several different corporate boards of directors is termed

    a. the power elite.
    b. interlocking directorships.
    c. multinationals.
    d. integrated national elite.

13. _____ is/are based on the private ownership of the means of production, hired workers, and commercial markets that are today increasingly international as well as domestic.

    a. Capitalism
    b. Monarchies
    c. Mixed economies
    d. Social democracies

14. Allocating formal power solely on the basis of heredity, _____ is/are the oldest type of authoritarian regime.

    a. dictatorships
    b. totalitarianism
    c. monarchies
    d. terrorist occupation

15. _____ is a type of authoritarianism in which there are no formal limits whatsoever on the extent to which the government can intervene in people's everyday lives.

    a. A dictatorship
    b. A monarchy
    c. Patrimonial regime
    d. Totalitarianism

16. _____ routinely include citizens in government and their consent is the formal basis for the legitimacy of the state.

    a. Democracies
    b. Totalitarianism
    c. Patrimonial regimes
    d. Monarchies

17. In a _____ democracy, citizens are personally involved in decision making.

    a. representative
    b. real
    c. participatory
    d. idealistic

18. All around the world today, authoritarian regimes are undergoing the transition from authoritarianism to democracy. This process is termed

    a. democratization.
    b. an elite pact.
    c. representation
    d. democide

19. The use or threat of violence as a political strategy by an individual, group, or state is termed

    a. democratic force.
    b. terrorism.
    c. hostile representation.
    d. democide.

20. In contrast to the American system, most representative democracies, especially in Western Europe, have _____ voting.

    a. persuasive
    b. nonproportional
    c. proportional
    d. percentage

TRUE-FALSE

1. Hispanic Americans are the fastest growing minority in the United States.

2. Sociologists use the term *political economy* in referring to the methods used by the current president in distributing scarce resources.

3. The *state* is the institution that organizes the production, distribution, and consumption of material goods and services.

4. Intellectuals are seldom the architects of utopian ideas.

5. The core values of classical liberalism focused on the rights of the individual, who was seen as ultimately autonomous from society and capable of reason.

6. As a philosophy, *conservatism* emphasizes social order and sees the family, religion, and the local face-to-face community as the natural bases for that order.

7. The ruling class thesis maintains that the upper class dominates the political economy of the capitalist countries despite occasional challenges by the working and middle classes.

8. The state autonomy thesis maintains that real power is concentrated in the hands of a small group of bureaucratic elites.

9. French sociologist Émile Durkheim was the major architect of the *power elite thesis*.

10. According to state autonomy theory, top government officials and policy experts play the key role in the development of policy.

ANSWERS - MULTIPLE CHOICE (correct answer/page reference)

1. b 462
2. c 462
3. d 462
4. a 463-464
5. d 464
6. c 465
7. b 467
8. a 468
9. b 468
10. d 469
11. c 469
12. b 471
13. a 474
14. c 475
15. d 476
16. a 476
17. c 476
18. a 476
19. b 478
20. c 480

ANSWERS - TRUE-FALSE (correct answer/page reference)

1. T 461
2. F 462
3. F 462
4. F 465
5. T 467
6. T 468
7. T 469
8. F 469
9. F 471
10. T 473

CHAPTER 18
HEALTH AND HEALTH CARE

LEARNING OBJECTIVES

➤ To understand the definition of health and how health is measured.

➤ To understand the figures used by social epidemiologists to track diseases.

➤ To discuss the link between culture and health.

➤ To compare and contrast health in the developing world with health in the developed world.

➤ To list and discuss the views of health espoused by the major sociological perspectives.

➤ To understand the impact of gender and race on mortality, morbidity, and mental health.

➤ To discuss the health care crisis in the U.S. as well as health care reform proposals.

CHAPTER OUTLINE

I. The Challenge of International Health
    A. World Patterns of Health and Disease
    B. Global Interdependence: Health and Technology

II. Sociological Perspectives on Health
    A. A Functionalist View of Health
    B. A Conflict View of Health
    C. Symbolic Interaction: The Social Construction of Health

SUMMARY

➤ The World Health Organization (WHO) defines health holistically, as a state of complete physical, mental, and social well being. Health is a fundamental human right.

➤ Health is often measured in terms of population's mortality rate (the percentage of people who die every year). Globally, the two most important indicators of health are the infant mortality rate (IMR) and the life expectancy rate at birth (LER).

➤ Epidemiology is the study of the causes and distribution of disease and disability in a given population. Epidemiologists are concerned with both the incidence of disease (the number of new cases reported over time) and the prevalence of disease (the total number of cases per period).

➤ Culture and economic development have an enormous impact on health. Infant mortality rates are much higher, and life expectancy is much lower, in developing countries than in developed nations, due mainly to poverty and a high rate of population growth.

➤ In both developed and developing nations, radiation and pollution have been linked to increases in cancer and immune deficiency diseases.

➤ Functionalists view disease as a symptom of disequilibrium in the social system. Emile Durkheim thought unhealthy behaviors like suicide were caused by a lack of social support; Talcott Parsons saw social support as an essential underpinning for the role of the sick person.

➤ Conflict theorists stress the relationship between social class and health. The high social position doctors enjoy gives them a great deal of power over the definition of disease and the delivery of health care, while people of low social class are more likely to become ill, and less likely to receive care, than people of higher social class.

➤ Symbolic interactionists see health as a social concept, and sickness as a role that is socially negotiated. The labeling of conditions as illness, the faith patients place in the care they receive, and the way doctors relate to patients are all socially constructed.

➤ Mortality is affected by gender and race—women tend to live longer than men, and whites to live longer than African Americans. But socioeconomic status has the strongest influence on mortality rates: the lower the status, the higher the mortality rate.

➢ As a group, women tend to suffer more from disease than men, though their mortality rate is lower. While race appears to affect disease rates, socioeconomic status is clearly a stronger influence.

➢ About 15 percent of Americans suffer from severe mental illness, which like other disease is more prevalent among people of lower socioeconomic status. By itself, gender does not seem to affect the prevalence of mental illness, but together with marital status, it does: married women are at greater risk for mental illness than married men.

➢ Though the United States spends a greater percentage of its gross domestic product on health care than any other nation, millions of Americans do not have health insurance. Health care is effectively rationed to those who are insured or who can pay for the care themselves on a fee-for-service basis.

➢ Medicare is a government health-insurance program that serves the elderly and people with disabilities. Medicaid is a welfare program that provides medical assistance to low-income people of all ages.

➢ Specialization of medical personnel, increased reliance on expensive technology, and a fragmented, uncoordinated system of competing providers are driving up health care costs in the United States and hampering efforts to provide patients with holistic health care.

➢ Efforts to contain rising medical costs, such as the move toward managed care, have for the most part failed, and have in many cases had a negative impact on patient care. The Clinton administration's proposal for national health care reform, which was based on the concept of managed competition among existing providers, was defeated by a coalition of special-interest groups.

MULTIPLE CHOICE

1. The World Health Organization defines *health* as

   a. the absence of disease.
   b. a state of complete physical, mental, and social well-being.
   c. the absence of infirmity.
   d. both a and c above

2. The World Health Organization's view of health is best described as

    a.   myopic.
    b.   singularly focused.
    c.   holistic.
    d.   concentrating only on disease and infirmity.

3. Population growth or decline, age, sex, birth and death rate, marital status, and ethnicity are all referred to sociologically as _____ characteristics.

    a.   demographic
    b.   morbidity
    c.   mortality
    d.   epidemiological

4. A percentage of the total number of deaths over the population size (X 1000) in a given time period, usually a year, is termed the _____ rate.

    a.   morbidity
    b.   demographic
    c.   epidemiological
    d.   mortality

5. The amount of disease or illness in a population is referred to as the

    a.   mortality rate.
    b.   epidemiological incidence.
    c.   demographic gap.
    d.   morbidity rate.

6. The number of deaths in the first year of life for each 1,000 live births is termed the

    a.   life expectancy rate.
    b.   infant mortality rate.
    c.   epidemiological incidence.
    d.   refined fertility rate.

7. _____ is the study of the causes and distribution of disease and disability in a given population.

    a.   Demography
    b.   Morbidity
    c.   Epidemiology
    d.   Gerontology

8. The _____ of disease refers to the number of new cases during a specified period of time.

    a. incidence
    b. prevalence
    c. epidemiology
    d. demography

9. The _____ of disease refers to the total number of cases during a specified time.

    a. incidence
    b. prevalence
    c. epidemiology
    d. demography

10. In every country of the developed world except for the United States, the organized social response to the process of health care transition has been translated into

    a. revolution.
    b. social turmoil.
    c. massive protest.
    d. national health insurance.

11. Which of the following is NOT one of Durkheim's types of suicide?

    a. anomic
    b. altruistic
    c. passive
    d. egoistic

12. Talcott Parsons used the term _____ in describing those behaviors which are socially expected of a sick person according to prevailing norms.

    a. sick role
    b. acute response
    c. chronic response
    d. anomie

13. _____ disease is characterized by sudden onset, rapid peak, and limited duration, resulting in either recovery or death.

   a. Chronic
   b. Episodic
   c. Epidemiological
   d. Acute

14. _____ disease is characterized by gradual onset, long duration, little chance for complete recovery, and often resulting in death.

   a. Chronic
   b. Episodic
   c. Non-episodic
   d. Acute

15. The process of _____ legitimizes medical control over parts of a person's life.

   a. encroachment
   b. epidemiology
   c. medicalization
   d. the sick role

16. The poor and the elderly are often prevented from receiving medical treatment because health care is rendered on what basis?

   a. third-party payer
   b. single-party payer
   c. fee-for-service
   d. as need demands

17. Enacted in 1965 during the presidency of Lyndon B. Johnson, _____ is a health insurance program funded through Social Security primarily for those age 65 and over, but with provisions for covering people of any age who have certain disabilities.

   a. Medicaid
   b. Medicare
   c. HMO
   d. third-party payer

18. _____ is a joint federal and state welfare program which provides medical assistance for certain individuals of any age with very low income.

    a.   HMO
    b.   Medicare
    c.   National health care insurance
    d.   Medicaid

19. _____ is a prepaid health plan offering complete medical services where physicians and other providers are either independently contracted or salaried employees.

    a.   Medicare
    b.   Medicaid
    c.   A health maintenance organization (HMO)
    d.   Third-party payer

20. The rise of HMOs marks a trend in health care delivery in the United States referred to as

    a.   managed care.
    b.   third-party payer.
    c.   single-party payer.
    d.   fee-for-service.

TRUE-FALSE

1. The text points out that it is easier to quantify health than disease.

2. About 80 percent of the world's population relies on health forms the West would refer to as "alternative."

3. The name Chernobyl is now synonymous with environmental purity.

4. Females outlive males in developed nations, but not in developing countries.

5. People of low socioeconomic status (SES) have higher morbidity rates for almost every disease or illness, especially in terms of higher rates of infectious and parasitic diseases and major mental disorders.

6. Regarding the demographics of mental illness, the most consistent finding is that there is a inverse relationship between mental illness and socioeconomic status (SES).

7. The *drift hypothesis* suggests that socioeconomic status (SES) deteriorates because of the presence of mental illness.

8. The percentage of Americans with no health insurance has declined dramatically.

9. The non-system model of health care is consistent with a conflict perspective.

10. President Bill Clinton's Health Security Act of 1993 has been a huge success.

ANSWERS - MULTIPLE CHOICE (correct answer/page reference)

1.	b	488
2.	c	488-489
3.	a	490
4.	d	490
5.	d	490
6.	b	491
7.	c	491
8.	a	491
9.	b	491
10.	d	495-496
11.	c	497-498
12.	a	498
13.	d	498
14.	a	498
15.	c	500
16.	c	511
17.	b	512
18.	d	513
19.	c	514
20.	a	514-515

<u>ANSWERS - TRUE-FALSE</u> (correct answer/page reference)

1.	F	489
2.	T	493
3.	F	497
4.	F	505
5.	T	508
6.	T	508
7.	T	509
8.	F	510
9.	T	514
10.	F	515

CHAPTER 19
RECREATION: AN EMERGING INSTITUTION

LEARNING OBJECTIVES

➤ To list the functions of media and sport in our society.

➤ To understand the conflict view of media and sport.

➤ To discuss the role of symbolic interactionism in studying recreational activities.

➤ To discuss the role and impact of mass media in the U.S.

➤ To understand the connections between sport and class, sport and religion, and sport and media.

➤ To discuss the negative aspects of media and sport.

CHAPTER OUTLINE

I.   Sociological Perspectives on Recreation
    A.   The Functions of Media and Sport
    B.   The Conflict View of Media and Sport
    C.   Symbolic Interactionism and Cultural Studies

SUMMARY

➤ Popular culture, including sport and the media, is an important component of the emerging institution of recreation.

➤ Early studies of the media often used the hypodermic model, which incorrectly suggests that the media's effects on their audiences are direct rather than mediated.

➤ The media and sport serve various functions, including providing employment, entertainment, and information; encouraging sociability; contributing to socialization; reinforcing social control; and promoting individual and cultural identity.

- ➤ Conflict theorists believe that the media perpetuate stereotypes and defend the interests of the powerful. They also argue that sport exploits and dehumanizes athletes, overemphasizes winning, stresses commercialism, and encourages excessive nationalism.

- ➤ Symbolic interactionists and cultural studies theorists focus on how the meaning of popular culture is constructed. Applied to sport, this approach draws attention to issues such as the development of gender roles and the use of Native American mascots.

- ➤ Watching television is a passive experience. New technologies have the potential to make it more active, but they are not being widely used to this end.

- ➤ Minorities have made considerable progress in Hollywood but women may be losing ground there.

- ➤ Popular music is youth oriented, often linked with movements for social change, and has become more mainstream.

- ➤ Sport is an intermediate category between play and spectacle. It is enormously popular in the United States and in many ways may be regarded as a microcosm of our society.

- ➤ People in different classes participate in and watch different sports. Most research suggests that sport participation is loosely linked with upward social mobility.

- ➤ Religions often use sport to attract support. Conversely, sport can be seen as a functional equivalent of religion with its own sacred rituals, heroes, and shrines.

- ➤ The media and sport enjoy an unequal symbiotic relationship in which sport depends more on the media than the media do on sport.

- ➤ Government rarely censors the media in the United States because the popular culture industries have developed voluntary rating systems.

- ➤ Sport frequently promotes aggressive and violent behavior. It also encourages such forms of deviance as the use of illicit performance-enhancing drugs.

- ➤ African Americans have made considerable progress in gaining equal treatment in sports, although subtle forms of discrimination such as stacking still exist. Opportunities for women have also expanded greatly as gender stereotypes have begun to fade. However, neither minorities nor women have greatly increased their involvement in coaching or sports administration.

MULTIPLE CHOICE

1. Commercialized art and entertainment designed to attract a mass audience is referred to as

   a. the mass media.
   b. the social message.
   c. popular culture.
   d. recreation.

2. In the course of modernization, the nations of the West became _____ characterized by large-scale economic production and numerous complex organizations.

   a. normless
   b. mass societies
   c. anomic
   d. hypodermic

3. The _____ model assumes that the media have a simple, one-way, direct effect on their audience.

   a. hypodermic
   b. institutional
   c. demographic
   d. medium-is-the-message

4. Which of the following is NOT one of the functions of media and sport discussed in the text?

   a. creating jobs
   b. encouraging sociability
   c. social control
   d. fostering a spectator spirit

5. Conflict theory suggests that the emerging institution of recreation tends to

   a. vitalize society and encourage its members to be more analytical.
   b. arouse the common people and motivate them to resist the efforts of the powerful to control them.
   c. reproduce the status quo and discourage social change.
   d. be informative, insightful, and philosophical.

6.	The value that winning is the only relevant goal in sport is often referred to as the

	a.	Lombardi ethic.
	b.	General Patton syndrome.
	c.	P.T. Barnum motif.
	d.	Joe Montana tradition.

7.	The text observes that when we see athletes perform well on the field and win, and when the media constantly associate winning with virtue, we generalize that people who are good in one area of life–in this case sports–must be *generally* good people. This phenomenon is known as the _____ effect.

	a.	Hawthorne
	b.	halo
	c.	glowing
	d.	winning

8.	Which perspective is fast becoming the sociological paradigm of choice for studying recreational activities, particularly the media and sports?

	a.	functionalism
	b.	conflict
	c.	symbolic interactionism
	d.	developmentalism

9.	_____ is a new interdisciplinary field, rooted in philosophy and the humanities which studies popular culture.

	a.	Existentialism
	b.	Holism
	c.	Ethnography
	d.	Cultural studies

10.	Which of the following is NOT mentioned in the text as among of the major commercial media?

	a.	the Internet
	b.	television
	c.	film
	d.	popular music

11. According to sociologist Jay Coakley's definition, *sport* is a concept halfway between play and

    a. game.
    b. imitation.
    c. spectacle.
    d. business.

12. A group of friends tossing a frisbee around the backyard is most illustrative of

    a. game.
    b. play.
    c. spectacle.
    d. sport.

13. About _____ percent of the American public is involved in sports, either as participants, as spectators, or in both roles.

    a. 60
    b. 70
    c. 80
    d. 90

14. Thorstein Veblen saw elite sports participation such as golf, tennis, yachting, skiing, and polo, as activity undertaken to validate the social status of the upper class by demonstrating that they could afford to throw money away on nonessentials. In Veblen's view, these activities are classic examples of

    a. anomie.
    b. class conflict.
    c. normative consensus.
    d. conspicuous consumption.

15. Gary Fine's study of Little League baseball identified four main value-themes. Which of the following is NOT one of these?

    a. personal effort
    b. sportsmanship
    c. selfishness
    d. winning and losing

16. According to the text's discussion of sport and the media,

    a.   the flow of media dollars has served to increase player salaries
    b.   the number of team franchises has expanded
    c.   television has largely killed off minor league sports
    d.   all of the above

17. The latest development in the "censorship wars" is a device that allows parents to block the reception of programs they don't want their children to watch. This technology is referred to as the

    a.   v-chip.
    b.   x-rated block.
    c.   scrambler box.
    d.   child protector.

18. Research on steroid use suggests that _____ percent of NFL players have used these drugs.

    a.   55
    b.   65
    c.   75
    d.   95

19. In a practice called _____, minorities are disproportionately assigned to "noncentral" positions which are low in outcome control and leadership responsibility.

    a.   tracking
    b.   stacking
    c.   blockbusting
    d.   redlining

20. Title _____ of the Educational Amendments Act of 1972 mandates that, in order to receive federal financial assistance, schools provide substantially equal athletic opportunities to both genders.

    a.   VI
    b.   VII
    c.   VIII
    d.   IX

TRUE-FALSE

1. Conflict theorists maintain that sports generally benefit women more than men, minorities more than whites, and the working class more than the elite.

2. Well over 95 percent of American homes have at least one television set, and it is turned on an average of seven hours each day.

3. The music industry is far more change-oriented than Hollywood.

4. Despite First Amendment guarantees of the freedom of speech, the United States has a long tradition of censoring unpopular ideas and graphic content.

5. In practice, the government has rarely directly acted as a censor, because the motion picture, television, and popular music industries voluntarily developed their own rating systems.

6. Most sociologists today believe that violence is innate rather than learned.

7. Before the Second World War, American sports were almost completely segregated with the exception of boxing.

8. Research shows that marginal minority players are more likely to be successful in college and professional sports than marginal whites.

9. Women began to participate regularly in organized sports in the early 19th century.

10. By 1990, nearly 50 percent of all collegiate women's teams were coached by women.

ANSWERS - MULTIPLE CHOICE (correct answer/page reference)

1.	c	520
2.	b	520
3.	a	520
4.	d	521-523
5.	c	523-524
6.	a	524
7.	b	524-525
8.	c	525
9.	d	525

10.	a	527
11.	c	530
12.	b	530
13.	b	530
14.	d	531
15.	c	532-533
16.	d	534-535
17.	a	536
18.	c	537
19.	b	537
20.	d	539

ANSWERS - TRUE-FALSE (correct answer/page reference)

1.	F	524
2.	T	527
3.	T	529
4.	T	535
5.	T	536
6.	F	536
7.	T	537
8.	F	538
9.	F	539
10.	T	540

CHAPTER 20
POPULATION, URBANIZATION, AND THE ENVIRONMENT

LEARNING OBJECTIVES

➤ To understand the differences between the major demographic tools: crude birth rate, fertility rate, and migration rate.

➤ To discuss the demographic transition model.

➤ To be able to express population trends in terms of the major sociological perspectives.

➤ To discuss the differences between urbanization in the developing world and urbanization in the developed world.

➤ To describe the contributions of Wirth and Redfield to the understanding of urbanization.

➤ To discuss the impact of population growth and industrial expansion on the environment, as well as strategies to counteract negative effects.

➤ To be able to understand the fate of the Amercian city, its past, and its future.

➤ To describe the concept of sustainable development, especially regarding the role of cities and the status of women.

CHAPTER OUTLINE

I.   Population: Demographic Interdependence
    A.   Studying Population: Demographic Tools
    B.   Understanding Development: The Demographic Transition
    C.   Explaining Population Trends: Sociological Theory

II.   Urbanization: Living in Global Communities
    A.   Global Urbanization
    B.   Urbanism as a Way of Life
    C.   Explaining Urban Trends: Sociological Theory
    D.   Symbols and Urbanization

III. Environment: Ecological Interdependence
    A.   The Game of Ecopolitics
    B.   Strategies for Environmental Success

SUMMARY

➢ Demography is the scientific study of the size, distribution, and composition of population over time. To account for changes in population, demographers study the fertility rate—the annual number of births to women of childbearing age—as well as other birth, death, and migration rates.

➢ In Europe and North America, the Industrial Revolution caused a profound drop in fertility and mortality rates and a corresponding increase in life expectancy, an effect that is referred to as the demographic transition. Today, the countries of the developing world are undergoing a similar process of industrialization and demographic change.

➢ In his *Essay on the Principles of Population* (1798), Thomas Malthus predicted that population growth would eventually outstrip agricultural production, causing widespread famine and death. Malthus was pessimistic about people's ability to change their reproductive behavior in response to diminishing resources.

➢ Emile Durkheim saw population growth as an incentive for the development of more efficient means of production through specialization and the division of labor. Durkheim stressed people's resourcefulness and adaptability in response to demographic change.

➢ Rather than population growth, Karl Marx stressed the unequal distribution of resources in a capitalist economic system as the cause of food shortages. Like Marx, modern-day conflict theorists and dependency theorists emphasize the maldistribution of resources and the economic dependency of the poor on the rich.

➢ About half the world's population lives in urban areas. While the developed world is at present more urbanized than developing countries, cities in Asia, Africa, and Latin America are the fastest growing places in the world.

➢ Both population increase and migration from impoverished rural areas are contributing to the growth of the world's cities. Globally, these centers of population growth and economic activity are becoming increasingly interconnected.

➢ Sociologists Louis Wirth and Robert Redfield wrote that, compared to intimate rural communities, cities tend to foster impersonal and distant social relations. In functionalist terms, though city dwellers seek a sense of community in formal and voluntary associations, their residence in urban areas puts them at risk for normlessness and alienation.

➤ Job loss is a major cause of breakdowns in the social fabric of the inner cities. Yet residents of many urban neighborhoods have managed to maintain a strong sense of community despite severe economic problems.

➤ Sociologist Robert Park founded the subfield of urban ecology on the principle that in urban areas, population density increases the competition for scarce land. Park thought that in all cities, urban growth would radiate outward from a central business district, but he did not foresee the modern-day trends toward decentralization and suburbanization.

➤ Though industrialization benefits society by increasing people's life chances, it has also degraded the environment, jeopardizing the health and well-being of communities around the world. Developing countries, with their limited resources and rapidly growing population, face a difficult tradeoff between social needs and environmental protection.

➤ In the United States, the most important population trend is the flight to the suburbs, where half the urban population now lives. The trend is threatening the viability of cities by depriving them of jobs and taxes, undermining housing and education in the process.

➤ Sustainable development is a concept that marries the goal of continuing economic development with the need to preserve the environment.

➤ Improving the status of women is the single most effective way to slow global population growth. The better educated women are, and the higher their status in the family and society, the more likely they are to limit the size of their families through contraception and family planning.

MULTIPLE CHOICE

1. _____ is the scientific study of population that focuses on its size, distribution, and composition, and how birth, death, and migration rates influence each element.

   a. Tomography
   b. Demography
   c. Urbanography
   d. Envirology

2. When a population is fully counted and measured according to key characteristics, we refer to the results as a/an

    a. demographic count.
    b. tomographic analysis.
    c. census.
    d. urban survey.

3. The most common measure of birth is the _____ rate, measuring the annual number of births per 1,000 population.

    a. fertility
    b. demographic
    c. fecundity
    d. crude birth

4. The _____ rate refers to actual reproductive behavior determined by the annual number of live births per 1,000 to women of childbearing age.

    a. fertility
    b. fecundity
    c. crude birth
    d. demographic

5. The movement of people in and out of various areas, specifically tracked according to political boundaries, is termed the

    a. demographic rate.
    b. migration rate.
    c. fertility rate.
    d. fecundity rate.

6. The _____ is a three stage model that describes the change from high fertility and mortality rates to lower ones.

    a. demographic gap
    b. refined fertility quotient
    c. demographic transition
    d. census count

7. A _____ is a figure that provides the age-and-sex structure of a population at a given point in time.

    a. demographic gap
    b. demographic transition
    c. migration quotient
    d. population pyramid

8. _____ suggests that if most young people marry and each married couple has two children, the population would replace itself and the growth rate would remain static.

    a. The demographic gap
    b. The demographic transition
    c. Zero Population Growth
    d. A population pyramid

9. Simply stated, the word _____ means a place of settlement, often called a city, that is populated more densely than rural areas.

    a. urban
    b. metropolis
    c. megalopolis
    d. globalization

10. _____ is the process of city population growth.

    a. Globalization
    b. Urbanization
    c. Metropolitanism
    d. Suburbanization

11. _____ are centers of population growth, political action, and economic activities that are becoming the dominant force in national and world economies.

    a. Urban places
    b. Suburban enclaves
    c. Metropolitan centers
    d. Global cities

12. _____ is a field interested in determining the relationships between urban populations and their physical and spatial environments.

    a.   Urban ecology
    b.   Metropolitan studies
    c.   Global studies
    d.   Megalopolitan studies

13. The phenomenon of *global warming* is also referred to as the _____ effect.

    a.   ionization
    b.   pressure
    c.   greenhouse
    d.   atomic

14. In the mid-twentieth century the _____ revolution was the term given to the industrial and technological innovations used to produce high-yield crops that would solve the world's food supply problem.

    a.   blue
    b.   green
    c.   yellow
    d.   brown

15. A _____ is a central city and surrounding smaller cities that function as an integrated economy.

    a.   metropolitan area
    b.   suburb
    c.   Metropolitan Statistical Area
    d.   Consolidated Metropolitan Statistical Area

16. Smaller surrounding urban areas outside the political boundaries of the central city are termed

    a.   industrial parks.
    b.   pocket parks.
    c.   demographic outskirts.
    d.   suburbs.

17. A _____ is a system of several metropolitan areas and their surrounding suburbs that expand until they overlap.

   a.   Metropolitan Statistical Area
   b.   Consolidated Metropolitan Statistical Area
   c.   megalopolis
   d.   suburban area

18. The Census Bureau designates a _____ as a central city of at least 50,000 people and its adjacent urbanized areas.

   a.   metropolitan area
   b.   suburb
   c.   megalopolis
   d.   Metropolitan Statistical Area

19. When the largest Metropolitan Statistical Areas are grouped together, they become

   a.   metropolitan areas.
   b.   Consolidated Metropolitan Statistical Areas.
   c.   megalopoli.
   d.   suburbs.

20. _____ is a process of renovating specific working-class or poor neighborhoods to attract new affluent residents.

   a.   Gentrification
   b.   Suburbanization
   c.   Metropolitanization
   d.   Megalopolitanism

TRUE-FALSE

1. T Fertility rates in many parts of the world have not declined fast enough to stem population growth.

2. F Thomas Malthus referred to common diseases, epidemics, wars, plague, and famine as *negative checks*.

3. T About half the world's population live in urban areas, but the developed world is twice as urbanized as the developing world.

4. F The *urban bias* argument is that class conflict exists between foreign and national interests; between labor and capital.

5. T The *spatial mismatch hypothesis* refers to an already weakened social fabric that declines further as people who can afford to do so move out of deteriorating neighborhoods.

6. F The *concentric zone* model of urban growth is based on the evolution of cities from a central business district.

7. F The *sector concept* and the *multiple nuclei* model are based on the organization of industrial cities according to territories radiating outward from a central business district.

8. T The two most important direct causes of environmental destruction are population growth and industrial expansion.

9. T The most descriptive measure of urban decline is population loss–first in a central city and then in its municipal boundaries.

10. T Sustainable development requires international cooperation in finding humane ways for the human species to live on the planet indefinitely without risking the future of either the planet or its inhabitants.

ANSWERS - MULTIPLE CHOICE (correct answer/page reference)

1.	b	544
2.	c	544
3.	d	545
4.	a	545
5.	b	545
6.	c	546
7.	d	546
8.	c	547
9.	a	551
10.	b	551
11.	d	553
12.	a	555
13.	c	558
14.	b	561

15.	a	562
16.	d	562
17.	c	562
18.	d	562
19.	b	562
20.	a	566

ANSWERS - TRUE-FALSE (correct answer/page reference)

1.	T	546
2.	F	548
3.	T	551
4.	F	553
5.	T	555
6.	F	556
7.	F	556
8.	T	557
9.	T	564
10.	T	567

CHAPTER 21
ORGANIZATIONS AND THE SOCIOLOGY OF WORK

LEARNING OBJECTIVES

➤ To describe the types of formal organizations.

➤ To discuss the characteristics of bureaucracies as well as recent refinements of those descriptions.

➤ To describe modifications of Weber's model.

➤ To discuss job satisfaction and work motivation among workers.

➤ To describe the three sectors of the economy.

➤ To describe the primary labor market and the role of professionals.

➤ To discuss the secondary labor market and its problems.

➤ To understand important issues such as women in the work place, unemployment, alienation, and the rise of technology.

CHAPTER OUTLINE

I.   Formal Organizations and Bureaucracies
        A.   Types of Formal Organizations
        B.   Bureaucracy
        C.   Refining the Model

SUMMARY

➤ Formal organizations dominate many aspects of life in modern societies. There are three basic types of formal organizations: coercive and utilitarian organizations and voluntary associations.

➤ A bureaucracy is a special variety of formal organization designed to allow large numbers of people to accomplish routine tasks as efficiently as possible. Max Weber developed a widely used six-point ideal type of model of bureaucracy.

➤ Weber saw modern society moving toward ever greater levels of bureaucratic rationality.

➤ Real-life bureaucratic functioning is influenced by the internal structure that develops among bureaucratic employees and is frequently impeded by various bureaucratic dysfunctions.

➤ Scientific management and the human relations school were early efforts to respond to the inefficiencies of bureaucracies. More recent reform efforts include the anti-bureaucratic collective model, the Japanese model, and the humanized model.

➤ Levels of job satisfaction vary among different types of workers.

➤ Max Weber saw the intense work ethic associated with rational capitalism as an unintended consequence of doctrinal changes introduced during the Protestant reformation.

➤ Sociologists identify three sectors of the economy—primary, secondary, and tertiary—and two labor markets, primary and secondary.

➤ In recent decades, the number of jobs that are structured as professions has substantially increased.

➤ Real wages for many American workers, especially those in the secondary labor market, have been declining because of globalization and the weakening of the union movement.

➤ The contingency work force, temporary workers, part-time workers, and independent contractors, has been rapidly expanding.

➤ Women have entered the workplace in unprecedented numbers in recent years. Unfortunately, many encounter hostile organizational cultures, tokenism, and dead-end jobs.

➤ Structural unemployment continues to be a problem for both blue-collar workers and downsized executives.

➤ Many American workers experience high levels of what Marx called alienation, a feeling of powerlessness that comes from not being able to control or even influence one's working conditions.

➤ Modern computer technologies are opening up new opportunities for workers, such as telecommuting, but they also introduce potential threats, such as electronic surveillance.

MULTIPLE CHOICE

1.   A/an _____ organization is a special type of secondary group.

     a.   informal
     b.   dedicated
     c.   formal
     d.   specialized

2.   A/an _____ organization secures conformity through force and the threat of punishment.

     a.   voluntary
     b.   coercive
     c.   utilitarian
     d.   informal

3.   A prison is an example of which type of organization?

     a.   voluntary
     b.   utilitarian
     c.   coercive
     d.   informal

4.   Businesses and other _____ organizations generally prefer a less costly way to obtain compliance: They reward their employees with money and other valued goods and privileges.

     a.   utilitarian
     b.   voluntary
     c.   coercive
     d.   informal

5.   _____ associations use *normative power*–that is, they secure almost limitless obedience by pursuing goals to which their members are personally committed.

     a.   Utilitarian
     b.   Coercive
     c.   Informal
     d.   Voluntary

6. Most contemporary formal organizations take the form of

    a. voluntary associations.
    b. bureaucracies.
    c. utilitarian organizations.
    d. coercive organizations.

7. A description that emphasizes, even exaggerates, a phenomenon's most distinctive or characteristic qualities is called a/an

    a. ideal type.
    b. division of labor.
    c. table of organization.
    d. formal operation.

8. Like all bureaucracies, universities are expected to be _____, hiring and promoting solely on the basis of specialized skills and knowledge.

    a. hierarchies
    b. formalized
    c. meritocracies
    d. partial

9. When a new problem arises, bureaucrats sometimes keep their heads down and avoid making adaptive decisions. Thorstein Veblen referred to this problem as

    a. trained incapacity.
    b. bureaucratic ritualism.
    c. Parkinson's Law.
    d. the bureaucratic personality.

10. Bureaucrats can become so committed to obeying official guidelines that the rules, in effect, become the organization's ends, even when such behavior ultimately blocks attainment of the group's real goals. This is the familiar problem of "red tape" or

    a. trained incapacity.
    b. goal succession.
    c. Parkinson's Law.
    d. bureaucratic ritualism.

11. Under some circumstances, an organization may devote most of its attention to simple survival rather than to achieving its ends. This illustrates the process of

    a.   goal succession.
    b.   goal displacement.
    c.   Parkinson's Law.
    d.   trained incapacity.

12. _____ states that work in a bureaucracy expands to fill the time available for its completion.

    a.   The Peter principle
    b.   The iron law of oligarchy
    c.   Parkinson's Law
    d.   Goal displacement

13. When bureaucrats are promoted until they reach their "level of incompetence," this illustrates

    a.   the Peter principle.
    b.   Parkinson's Law.
    c.   goal displacement.
    d.   the iron law of oligarchy.

14. Even if their members are ideologically and personally committed to running the organization democratically, bureaucracies often succumb to what political scientist Robert Michels called

    a.   goal displacement.
    b.   goal succession.
    c.   the iron law of oligarchy.
    d.   trained incapacity.

15. The _____ sector of the economy includes jobs in which material goods are obtained directly from nature (e.g., farming, mining, and fishing).

    a.   quarternary
    b.   tertiary
    c.   secondary
    d.   primary

16. Manufacturing industries make up which sector of the economy?

    a. primary
    b. secondary
    c. tertiary
    d. quaternary

17. Services make up which sector of the economy?

    a. primary
    b. secondary
    c. tertiary
    d. quaternary

18. _____ results from a mismatch between the skills of the work force and the current needs of the economy.

    a. Structural unemployment
    b. Organizational culture
    c. Alienation
    d. Underemployment

19. _____ are working but at jobs that do not make full use of their skills.

    a. Discouraged workers
    b. The structurally unemployed
    c. The underemployed
    d. Organizational employees

20. In Karl Marx's view, _____ arises whenever people are controlled by social institutions that seem beyond their ability to influence.

    a. revolution
    b. conflict
    c. dysfunction
    d. alienation

TRUE-FALSE

1. Bureaucracies are a relatively new phenomenon.

2. By *rationality*, Weber means consciously using the most effective means to pursue a chosen end.

3.   The actual character of an organization is always a sort of *negotiated order*.

4.   The evolution of the March of Dimes is a classic example of *goal succession*.

5.   *Quality circles* are techniques that management uses to dominate employees.

6.   *Occupational encapsulation* refers to workers becoming so specialized that they are inefficient.

7.   Primary labor market jobs are good jobs.

8.   Jobs in the secondary labor market are bad jobs.

9.   Sociologically, a *profession* is a prestigious white-collar occupation.

10.   Workers who are not permanent, full-time employees of a single firm are part of what is called the *contingency work force*.

ANSWERS - MULTIPLE CHOICE (correct answer/page reference)

1.	c	576
2.	b	576
3.	c	576
4.	a	576
5.	d	576
6.	b	577
7.	a	577
8.	c	578
9.	a	581
10.	d	581
11.	b	581
12.	c	581
13.	a	581-582
14.	c	582
15.	d	589
16.	b	589
17.	c	589
18.	a	596
19.	c	596
20.	d	597

ANSWERS - TRUE-FALSE (correct answer/page reference)

1. F   577
2. T   578
3. T   580
4. T   581
5. F   585
6. F   586
7. T   590
8. T   590
9. F   590
10. T   593

CHAPTER 22
COLLECTIVE BEHAVIOR AND SOCIAL MOVEMENTS

LEARNING OBJECTIVES

➢ To list and describe the five major theories explaining collective behavior.

➢ To discuss the difference between localized and dispersed collectives and give examples of each.

➢ To describe the theories attempting to explain why people join social movements.

➢ To be able to understand the resource-mobilization theory.

➢ To distinguish between the three types of social movements: reformist, revolutionary, and reactionary.

➢ To describe the developmental steps of social movements.

➢ To discuss the major trends in movement development.

CHAPTER OUTLINE

I.   Collective Behavior
      A.   Explaining Collective Behavior
      B.   Forms of Collective Behavior

II.   Social Movements
      A.   Why Do People Join Social Movements?
      B.   Resource Mobilization Theory
      C.   The Political-Process Approach

SUMMARY

➢ Collective behavior arises in situations in which institutionalized norms appear inadequate because they are unclear or rapidly changing. It tends to be relatively short-lived, spontaneous, and unorganized.

➢ Contagion theory emphasizes the emotional dimensions of collective behavior. Convergence theory explains the similarity of crowd participants as a consequence of the fact that only certain types of people choose to participate in any particular episode of collective behavior.

➢ Neil Smelser's value-added theory identifies six factors that must be present if collective behavior is to occur: structural conduciveness, structural strain, a generalized belief, a precipitating incident, mobilization for action, and social control.

➢ Emergent-norm theory and the assembling perspective are modern theories of the origins of collective behavior.

➢ Crowds and panics are the major types of localized collectivities. There are five varieties of crowds: casual, conventional, expressive, acting, and protest.

➢ The major forms of dispersed collectivities include rumors; mass hysteria; disaster behavior; fashion, fads, and crazes and publics.

➢ Social movements are collective efforts to promote or resist change that use at least some relatively uninstitutionalized methods. They have traditionally been analyzed as a type of collective behavior.

➢ The formal organizations that promote the goals of social movements are known as SMOs. The level of movement activity in a society fluctuates over time.

➢ Mass-society theory, now generally discredited, suggests people join social movements to compensate for their own personal inadequacies.

➢ Relative-deprivation theory explains movement membership as a consequence of peoples feeling a negative discrepancy between their present situation and the circumstances to which they feel they are entitled.

➢ Modern explanations of movement membership focus on recruitment through interpersonal networks and the process of frame alignment.

➢ Resource-mobilization theory analyzes the origin and development of social movements in terms of their ability to obtain and make effective use of such resources as leadership, supporters, and access to the mass media.

➢ Political process theory is a macro-level approach that studies the relationship between social-movement development and the political and economic structure of the society where the movement arises.

➤ Reformist social movements work for relatively small-scale changes whereas revolutionary movements seek to change a society's fundamental economic, political, and stratification systems. Regressive social movements try to reverse the direction in which change is currently moving.

➤ Many social movements pass through a four-stage career or life cycle pattern of incipience, coalescence, bureaucratization, and decline.

➤ Today, social movements are becoming increasingly professionalized. But sociologists have also noticed the emergence of a new type of movement that is ideologically inclusive, global in scope, highly participatory, and emotional.

MULTIPLE CHOICE

1. Which of the following is NOT one of Neil Smelser's preconditions for collective behavior?

    a. class consciousness
    b. structural strain
    c. precipitating incident
    d. mobilization for action

2. Formally speaking, a *collectivity*

    a. is a well-organized group with clearly defined norms.
    b. is filled with solidarity.
    c. a substantial number of people who interact on the basis of loosely defined norms.
    d. generates considerable group loyalty and has clear boundaries.

3. _____ are temporary gatherings of people who influence each other in some way and share a focus of attention.

    a. Collectivities
    b. Groups
    c. Localized collectivities
    d. Crowds

4. The simplest form of collective behavior is probably the _____ crowd.

    a. conventional
    b. casual
    c. expressive
    d. acting

5.	_____ crowds grow out of relatively structured gatherings such as parades, sports events, and funerals.

	a.	Casual
	b.	Expressive
	c.	Conventional
	d.	Protest

6.	On occasion, people deliberately seek out collective behavior experiences because they are an enjoyable way to release our emotions. These gatherings may be called _____ crowds.

	a.	expressive
	b.	conventional
	c.	casual
	d.	acting

7.	When the dominant emotion in a crowd is anger, and its attention is focused outward, we speak of which kind of crowd?

	a.	casual
	b.	conventional
	c.	expressive
	d.	acting

8.	Unlike a mob, a _____ is an acting crowd that directs its hostility toward a wide and shifting range of targets, moving from one to the next in a relatively unpredictable manner.

	a.	riot
	b.	gaggle
	c.	collectivity
	d.	protest crowd

9.	A _____ is a type of localized collective behavior in which a large number of people respond to a real or imaginary threat with a desperate, uncoordinated, seemingly irrational flight to secure safety.

	a.	protest crowd
	b.	collectivity
	c.	panic
	d.	riot

10. _____ is unverified information passed informally from person to person.

 a. A panic
 b. A rumor
 c. Gossip
 d. Mass hysteria

11. _____ consists of rumors about other people's personal affairs.

 a. Gossip
 b. Panic
 c. Mass hysteria
 d. Speculation

12. Periodic changes in the popularity of styles of hair, clothes, automobiles, architecture, music, sports, language, and even pets are termed

 a. crazes.
 b. fads.
 c. insanity.
 d. fashion.

13. _____ are shorter-lived than fashions, adopted briefly and enthusiastically and then quickly abandoned.

 a. Crazes
 b. Fads
 c. Fashion
 d. Publics

14. A _____ is simply a relatively long-lasting fad with significant economic or cultural implications.

 a. public
 b. fashion
 c. craze
 d. trend

15. A _____ is a relatively large and organized group of people working for or opposing social change and using at least some unconventional or uninstitutionalized methods.

    a. social movement
    b. fad
    c. craze
    d. fashion

16. A conscious feeling of a negative discrepancy between legitimate expectations and present actualities is termed

    a. micro mobilization.
    b. relative deprivation.
    c. frame alignment.
    d. resource mobilization

17. *Reformist movements*

    a. aim for large-scale and extremely progressive change.
    b. try to substantially alter society's basic political, economic, and stratification systems.
    c. attempt to reverse the general direction in which society is currently moving.
    d. none of the above

18. _____ movements seek broad and sweeping progressive changes, including alterations in society's economic and political institutions and system of stratification.

    a. Reformist
    b. Utopian
    c. Revolutionary
    d. Reactionary

19. Sometimes, people seek fundamental change not by directly challenging the existing system, but by withdrawing from it and creating their own alternative societies. These efforts reflect what type of movement?

    a. reactionary
    b. utopian
    c. revolutionary
    d. reformist

20. In the United States, the Ku Klux Klan, the militia movement, the Christian Right, and the pro-life movement are all examples of which type of movement?

   a. reactionary
   b. utopian
   c. revolutionary
   d. reformist

TRUE-FALSE

1. T Convergence theory argues that only certain kinds of people will be attracted by the opportunity to participate in a given episode of collective behavior.

2. T A mob is a highly emotional crowd that pursues a specific target, attacks it violently, and then fades away.

3. F Protest crowds are arbitrary and have no deliberate assembly or a leader.

4. T Urban legends are rumors that recount ironic and usually grisly events that supposedly happened to "a friend of a friend."

5. F Mass hysteria is very different from panic and involves a rational reaction to an imaginary threat.

6. F A public is a small or large number of people who are in direct contact with each other and may not be interested in the same controversial issues.

7. T Most social movements include a number of distinct formal organizations, referred to as social movement organizations.

8. F The *frame-alignment* approach is best characterized as a functionalist strategy.

9. T The pro-life movement is an example of a *countermovement*.

10. T In some cases, political leaders pursue a policy of *co-optation*, adopting watered-down versions of the changes advocated by a reformist movement and offering movement leaders rewarding positions within the power structure.

ANSWERS - MULTIPLE CHOICE (correct answer/page reference)

1. a 605
2. c 606
3. d 607
4. b 607
5. c 607
6. a 607
7. d 607
8. a 608
9. c 609
10. b 610
11. a 610
12. d 612
13. b 613
14. c 613
15. a 614
16. b 615
17. d 618
18. c 618
19. b 618
20. a 619

ANSWERS - TRUE-FALSE (correct answer/page reference)

1. T 605
2. T 607-608
3. F 609
4. T 611
5. F 611
6. F 613
7. T 614
8. F 615
9. T 619
10. T 621

CHAPTER 23
SOCIAL CHANGE AND DEVELOPMENT

LEARNING OBJECTIVES

➢   To be able to define social change and identify its sources.

➢   To discuss the four theories of social change.

➢   To compare and contrast Durkheim's, Marx's, and Weber's analyses of social change, including modern updates.

➢   To explain the relationship between foreign aid, economic development, and democracy in developing countries.

➢   To explain what is meant by a global economy, including discussions of the nations of the Pacific Rim and Africa.

➢   To discuss the tension between social change and tradition.

CHAPTER OUTLINE

I.   What is Social Change?

II.   Sources of Social Change
        A.   The Natural Environment
        B.   Demographic Changes
        C.   New Ideas
        D.   New Technologies
        E.   Government
        F.   Competition and War
        G.   Planned Change from Above
        H.   Social Movements

III.   The Great Transformation

IV.   Theoretical Perspectives on Social Change
        A.   Cyclical Theory
        B.   Evolutionary Theory
        C.   Functional Theory
        D.   Conflict Theory

V. Social Change in the Developed World: Theoretical Perspectives
    A. Updating Durkheim
    B. Updating Marx
    C. Updating Weber

VI. Social Change in the Developing World
    A. The Global Economy
    B. The Pacific Century
    C. The African Contrast
    D. The Informal Sector

SUMMARY

> Social change is a feature of all societies. However, its pace has increased dramatically over the past few centuries. Cultural change may take the form of invention, discovery, or diffusion. Resistance to change is motivated by cultural inertia and promoted by the actions of vested interests.

> Major sources of social change include the natural environment, demographic change, new ideas and technologies, government, competition and war, planning, and social movements.

> Over the past two hundred years, large parts of the world have undergone modernization. The fully developed nations are not moving into a postindustrial phase.

> Cyclical theory sees societies as moving through long-term, directional phases of growth and decay. Evolutionary theory suggests that societies tend to change in the direction of greater complexity and increased institutional differentiation.

> Classic functional theory interpreted most social change as an effort to restore systemic equilibrium. Conflict theory sees change as a natural consequence of struggles between competing groups for scare resources.

> Sociologists working in the Durkheimian tradition regard the rise of anomie and the consequent weakening of the social bond as a major problem of contemporary developed societies. The communitarian movement is an effort to respond to this challenge.

> Post-Marxist conflict theorists like Dahrendorf have redefined the problem of class struggle in terms of the broader concept of authority relations.

➤ George Ritzer, working in the Weberian tradition, sees McDonaldization as an extension of bureaucratic rationality.

➤ Foreign aid is provided to the developing world both out of humanitarian motives and as a stimulus to the growth of democracy and free-enterprise capitalism. NGOs and MNCs are important players in the process of international economic development.

➤ The nations of the Pacific Rim have been especially successful in the emerging global economy while most of those in the sub-Saharan Africa are lagging far behind.

➤ Microenterprise programs help people, especially women, in the developing world establish small businesses, particularly in the informal sector.

➤ Countermodern movements in Iran and Afghanistan have arisen in opposition to Westernization. They have had negative effects, especially on women, and apparently also on economic development.

➤ Female genital mutilation is a traditional practice endured by women in some parts of the developing world. A broad-based agreement that FGM is a human rights issue is developing.

➤ Recent international conferences have led to an emerging worldwide consensus concerning the importance of basic human rights.

MULTIPLE CHOICE

1. Social _____ refer(s) to alterations over time in social structure, culture, and behavior patterns.

   a. movements
   b. change
   c. turmoil
   d. functions

2. Sociologist Thorstein Veblen used which term to describe individual interests and groups whose advantages are threatened by impending social change?

   a. cultural inertia
   b. revolutionary forces
   c. vested interests
   d. change prospects

3. The view that technology is the only important source of social change is termed

   a. technological determinism.
   b. cultural inertia.
   c. immanent technology.
   d. post-modernism.

4. The sum total of the structural and cultural changes that accompanied the industrial revolution is referred to as

   a. modernity.
   b. post-modernism.
   c. cultural inertia.
   d. modernization.

5. The social changes associated with modernization have altered individual behavior patterns, creating a personal orientation termed

   a. modernity.
   b. post-modernism.
   c. postindustrialism.
   d. ideationalism.

6. In _____ society, manufacturing is largely replaced by knowledge-based service industries.

   a. industrial
   b. postindustrial
   c. intensive agricultural
   d. future

7. The difficulty of moving into the postindustrial era has stimulated the rise of a school of thought called

   a. modernity.
   b. modernization.
   c. postindustrialism.
   d. post-modernism.

8.	According to Pitirim Sorokin, in _____ eras, ultimate truth is believed to be discoverable through scientific research.

	a.	ideational
	b.	immanent
	c.	sensate
	d.	idealistic

9.	During _____ eras, Pitirim Sorokin indicated that people seek truth through the transcendent.

	a.	idealistic
	b.	ideational
	c.	sensate
	d.	immanent

10.	Pitirim Sorokin posited that, after centuries, the possibilities of one cultural pattern become exhausted and society inevitably shifts, occasionally to a/an _____ era.

	a.	idealistic
	b.	ideational
	c.	sensate
	d.	immanent

11.	The general trend of history is toward greater complexity and toward the development of more and more specialized institutional arrangements. This process is referred to as

	a.	idealism.
	b.	sensationalism.
	c.	institutional differentiation.
	d.	ideationalism.

12.	Herbert Spencer and his followers thought that all societies would ultimately follow the same evolutionary path. This approach to change is called _____ theory.

	a.	functional
	b.	conflict
	c.	interactionist
	d.	unilinear or evolutionary

13. Sociologists like Neil Smelser and Gerhard and Jean Lenski have modified evolutionary thinking: They have retained the idea that as societies grow, they *tend* to become more complex, institutionally different, and adaptive, but they reject the notion that change is necessarily progress and recognize that societies may change at different paces and in quite different ways. This approach is referred to as _____ theory

    a. multilinear evolutionary
    b. functional
    c. symbolic interactionist
    d. conflict

14. Robert Putnam theorizes that there has been a decline in the features of social organization, such as networks, norms, and social trust, that facilitate cooperation for mutual benefit. Putnam has referred to this process as a decline in

    a. institutional differentiation.
    b. social capital.
    c. idealism.
    d. functional prerequisites.

15. George Ritzer convincingly argues that modern societies are in the grip of an even more relentless rationalization process than Max Weber previously observed. Ritzer calls this trend

    a. the Burger King syndrome.
    b. Wendymania.
    c. McDonaldization.
    d. Taco Bellism.

16. The text observes that *nongovernmental organizations (NGOs)* are

    a. part of various governmental agencies.
    b. ineffective in looking after the interests of the poor.
    c. publically funded, profit-oriented groups.
    d. none of the above

17. _____ are large private business enterprises operating simultaneously in several countries.

    a. Nongovernmental organizations
    b. Capital states
    c. Multinational corporations
    d. Global economies

18. In practice, many less developed countries (LDCs) have adopted a model whereby public funds are extensively used to promote economic development, but the system remains responsive to market conditions. This model is termed

   a. state capitalism.
   b. functionalism.
   c. modified socialism.
   d. communism.

19. Earlier models of international economic interdependence have been replaced by the concept of a

   a. postindustrial society.
   b. global economy.
   c. information age.
   d. sensate era.

20. _____ movements resist certain aspects of modernization and also promote ways to neutralize their effects.

   a. Countermodern
   b. Anomic
   c. Social
   d. Terrorist

TRUE-FALSE

1. F Cultural inertia refers to extreme social pressures in the direction of revolutionary change.

2. T *Technologies* are tools and the skills needed to manufacture and use them.

3. T The primary causes of social change are believed by cyclic theorists to be immanent.

4. F Cyclic theory is more analytic than descriptive.

5. T Unilinear evolutionary theory has been criticized for not fitting the facts.

6. T Classic functionalism has been severely faulted for its implicit assumption that change is abnormal.

7. F Conflict theory acknowledges that change sometimes proceeds gradually and without much apparent conflict.

8. T Nations of the developing world are often referred to as *less developed countries (LDCs)*.

9. F Subsistence farmers and urban laborers who work in small-scale home-based production are part of the formal sector of the economy.

10. T *Microenterprise programs* involve small-scale income-earning manufacturing or agricultural activities located in or around the household.

ANSWERS - MULTIPLE CHOICE (correct answer/page reference)

1.	b	628
2.	c	629
3.	a	631
4.	d	632
5.	a	632
6.	b	632
7.	d	632
8.	c	633
9.	b	633
10.	a	634
11.	c	634
12.	d	634
13.	a	634
14.	b	636
15.	c	638
16.	d	640
17.	c	640
18.	a	641
19.	b	641
20.	a	646

ANSWERS - TRUE-FALSE (correct answer/page reference)

1. F   629
2. T   631
3. T   633
4. F   634
5. T   634
6. T   635
7. F   635
8. T   638
9. F   643
10. T   643